Road To Rishi Konda

Geetha Waters

First print book edition: Sydney, 2016.
Publisher: Sydney School of Arts & Humanities
15-17 Argyle Place
Millers Point NSW Australia
www.ssoa.com.au

ISBN: 978-0-9944199-9-6

Copyright © Geetha Waters, 2014. First published as an ebook 2014.

All rights reserved. Without limiting the rights under copyright reserved above, no part of this publication may be reproduced, stored in or introduced into a retrieval system, or transmitted, in any form or by any means (electronic, mechanical, photocopying, recording or otherwise), without the prior written permission of both the copyright owner and the publisher.

Dedication

For Christopher, my lifelong friend and companion, and both our parents, Gomathy & Velu Bharathan and Joan & Alan Waters.

Acknowledgements

My thanks go to the teaching communities of the Krishnamurti schools in India, Great Britain and the United States, as well as members of Krishnamurti Australia, including Jennifer Howe, Terry O' Brien and Gerald Reardon, for keeping alive the enquiry into holistic education. Thanks also to members of Our Memoir Group (OMG!) in Surry Hills, Sydney. I would like to make special mention of the inspiration I gained from Dorothy Simmons and Hilda and Harry Moorhead who assisted Jiddu Krishnamurti at his schools. I am grateful to Donald Ingram Smith, Mark Lee and Christine Williams who encouraged my writing, and Friedrich Grohe, Mary Zimbalist, Mary Keizer and Andrew Hilton for motivating me to stay with the project through decades of enquiry and self-reflection. My thanks to Jeremy Gilling for his proofreading skills. I am pleased to include the finely-crafted cover artwork and design by Cait Maloney and the expressive sketches by Augustin Tougas. I must also thank Chris Waters for my bio photograph, and my sons, Nicholas and Jayson, for providing me with countless opportunities for fun and learning throughout their lives.

Contents

Introduction	9
Edava	11
The Consulting Rooms	17
Land of Illusion	23
Learning From the Ground Up	26
A Rose by any other Name	32
Beloved of the Gods	36
The Sandalwood Tree	42
A Common Well	48
Salute	54
Dancing Sticks	58
Who is this I?	63
Freedom in the Hills	69
The Banyan Tree	76
Free Rangers	80
Role Play	85
Eavesdrop and Hoodwink	89
A Suitable School	95
Fledgling Love	100
And then there was Christopher	107
Christmas Day 1980	114
Notes	121

Introduction

Krishnamurti is widely known as a philosopher but I am interested in throwing light on his work as a revolutionary twentieth century educator. He would famously warn his students about the impact of conditioning and urge them to observe the impact of labels on their minds.

I grew up in an environment during the 1960s and 1970s that was intentionally created to liberate human intelligence from the authority of the known. How the Krishnamurti schools approached this problem of conditioning is a matter of some curiosity, and I have tried to capture the sense of growing up with a form of inquiry that has inspired me throughout my life. Thanks to Krishnamurti's holistic education at Rishi Valley School in Andhra Pradesh, I came to realise that using discourse and inquiry were pragmatic ways to understand how meaning is made as we engage with the world. Krishnamurti, or Krishnaji as we respectfully referred to him in India, made sure that the inquiry took place over the whole course of our education beginning from the early years, right through to the end of school.

Under his guidance, we students explored the movement of our thoughts and opinions. In seeing the difference between a word and the thing to which the word referred, I noticed how approximating the actual to an idea of it sets the scene for psychological unrest.

I believe that such subtle changes in perception are important for children to take note of before they become conditioned to rely on prior knowledge to explain the unfolding facts of their lives. As adults, we need to appreciate that children are sensitive and can see far more than we often give them credit for. They should be allowed opportunities for deep reflection and expression of their doubts, uncertainties and insights.

My hope is that this anthology of stories might stimulate others to question and discuss the issues that the character, Geetha, confronts as she grows through childhood into adolescence and womanhood. These issues – such as identity, relationship, what reality consists of, and the disparity between what people say and how they act – are encountered by all of us from our early years.

Geetha Waters

Edava

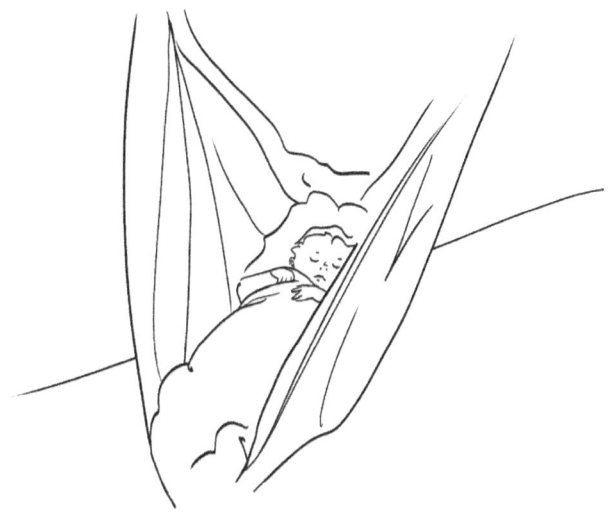

I was born in Varkala, in the state of Kerala on the west coast of South India. My maternal grandmother Kochu Parvathi lived about half an hour away in a rural area called Edava. This word can be translated as 'come hither' or 'come here' – and also, as I later imagined, could mean 'this voice', referring to my inner voice.

As an infant in the 1960s, I was closely bonded to my maternal grandmother and followed her voice everywhere, because my mother Gomathy (Amma) was a career woman and away from home during working hours. Amma had come first in the state for a national language test in the early 1940s when she was sixteen. My grandmother explained to me that because of my mother's exceptional score, she had been trained to be a Hindi teacher.

Hindi was the official language of India after independence. It was a northern language. The central government, based in New Delhi, wished to impose a language spoken largely in the north to unite a multilingual country under the banner of the largest democracy on earth. So my mother was part of that political move by the north to colonise the south.

They were exciting times, and Amma was thrilled to be part of such a bold and idealistic initiative after having lived through years of uncertainty and turbulence during the nationalists' attempt to rid the country of British rule. My grandmother said she was proud of her daughter – my mother – who was able to help with the household expenses. She was a modern woman who could look forward to being fully self-sufficient. She could even marry someone of her own choice.

After her training, my mother was recruited by the Kerala state government to teach languages at high school. She was fluent in Malayalam and Hindi, and could read and write in English, so her future was secure. She spent the rest of her life at first earning a teacher's salary, and after retirement on a family pension. Amma was independent, generous, witty and beautiful with dark curly hair. But she was rarely at home during the day.

However, my grandmother was always present. She had curly white hair, was ever so slim, soft-skinned, and wrinkled even when I was young. She wore a white cotton blouse with a deep cleavage which was tied in a knot under her small round breasts and a colourful sarong around her tiny waist. She was sprightly and erect, and moved purposefully around the house and garden. Her domain, the garden, was full of vegetables, herbs, gourds and edible roots growing under the canopy of palm fronds high above our heads. She was always calling me to 'come hither.' So I thought that Edava, the place where we lived, was named appropriately, in accordance with her direction!

I did not know my paternal grandmother, who died before I was born. She'd lived in Mayyanad, which was about twenty kilometres to the north of Edava. I was told that my father's mother had died during a cyclone while he was still a boy. During the storm, as winds swirled around their house, a beam which had been holding up the roof fell on her and broke her back. At the time she had four children, two boys and two girls.

My father and his older brother did what they could to look after their mother and younger siblings. Aunts and uncles had helped out until their father returned from Sri Lanka where he had been working on a white man's estate. He had to come by boat over the ocean and then overland across the Western Ghats to get back to Mayyanad. It had been a difficult journey and it had taken him eight weeks from the time he had received news of his wife's accident. On the day he arrived, my paternal grandmother entrusted her children to their father's care, and then she died. She had clung to life until he'd arrived, my father said, to make sure that her children would have someone reliable to take care of them.

After the funeral, the family split up. The girls remained with an aunt, my father's older brother was sent to Singapore with an uncle and my father went to live in Sri Lanka with my grandfather. There he worked as a servant until he was in his early teens. Then he went to find work at a college so he could learn to speak English. He had gone to see an Oxford graduate called Dr Hayman, who was the headmaster of St Thomas College at Gurutalawa. My father told him he would work at anything as long as he could learn to read and write. He began work in the gardens and learned a great deal about plants from the gardeners. For the first time in his life, he was working alongside people who were relaxed and respectful. He thought he was in heaven.

The children attending the college were from wealthy families and they went on wildlife excursions into the jungles. My father had the time of his life, even once being chased by a wild boar with sharp tusks. He said he hadn't realised he could run so fast until he had faced that threat of attack. Working at St Thomas College had changed his life. Gradually his English improved and he began to work at the headmaster's home, assisting around the house and working in the school when he had spare time.

In Singapore, my father's brother, Vasudevan, learned to sew to assist in his uncle's tailoring business. The two boys rarely met after that, even though they kept in touch by post, as their mother had entrusted them with the responsibility of taking care of their sisters. Together, they made enough money for a dowry for the girls and built themselves two houses in Mayyanad, close to where their family home had once stood. Land was cheap then, my father had said. Because the housing land was near the paddy fields, it had been designated as a flood zone. However, while my father was growing up in Sri Lanka, new fields were created upriver from his homelands, so they did not flood very often after all. His dream was to build himself a substantial home before he married. He had always planned to have children and he wanted to make sure that they would live in a solid house that would withstand the tempestuous weather of the tropics during monsoons. One of his sisters married a young man from Edava. My uncle, Vasudevan, had befriended the man in Singapore when he had begun thinking of settling down, so had introduced him to his sister who was a schoolteacher. The two brothers worked to make the wedding a grand affair, and many people came by train from the groom's home in Edava to Mayyanad for the occasion. New alliances were formed and soon there were many more weddings between different members of the two extended families.

My father and his brother married two sisters. They all agreed it was a perfect double match because the sisters would live close to each other and raise their families in Mayyanad while the men were overseas. Kamala, my mother's elder sister, had a beautiful daughter first and then a son who was eight months older than me. My mother had two girls. My parents named us Girija and Geetha. Years later, this was news to me, because we were both known by a generic term 'Kochu', which meant 'little one'. I liked the name because it sounded similar to my grandmother's name, Kochu Parvathi. My sister looked a lot like my grandmother and I was told that I looked like my grandfather. We had numerous other cousins to play with, who were all related in some way to either my father's people or my mother's, and sometimes they were related to both. Some of our conversations were devoted to finding out how our bloodlines crossed over. It was fascinating for me to hear how our elders had found each other, where they went to make a living and how their children had borrowed the looks of different relatives stretching back a few generations.

'The soil in Mayyanad is very porous. It is covered in sand and surrounded by ocean. The soil in Edava is rocky and full of minerals,' my grandmother would say. I was left to decipher this message as meaning that she was proud of the rich quality of the earth where she had always lived rather than where my father had chosen to build our home.

There had been forests along the coast when she was a little girl, around the turn of the twentieth century. As the decades passed, many of these forests had been cleared to plant coconut palms because that was the new cash crop of the time. She had seen the new railway lines being laid to connect places from one end of India to the other. That was the white man's plan to help with their trade routes. For centuries people in Kerala had been trading with the rest of the world from the port in Cochin. Kerala had been a quieter place back then. My grandmother explained that people had never succumbed to the pressure to cede to the British, the way the rest of India had. Keralans had maintained a thriving business relationship with the British and Portuguese, yet kept their autonomy.

'The British are ruled by a matriarch with a very high, haughty nose,' my grandmother explained. 'That's why they were so successful at whatever they did. But they did not stand a chance when it came to overpowering an ancient matriarchal culture such as here in Kerala.'

I listened to her, understanding only in part her musings about her own childhood and her children's marriages. She spoke of how the world had opened up during her lifetime and how so many people had gone abroad to make a living in faraway places. The soil here had remained the same, she said, looking at the ground with admiration. It was rocky and as rich as ever. The trees in her yard had grown tall and the palms were full of fruit. I would probably grow up later in a place called Andhra, she said, where my father was working.

My mother had told her about the people who lived there and the language they spoke. They were poor people who lived in a dry hilly place with very little rain. Unlike the people of Kerala, they were mostly illiterate. My mother was a brave and independent woman, travelling on her own with us on a two-day trip to visit our father in Andhra. If I wanted to, I could be a good teacher just like her, I was told. After all, I had the added advantage of the genes of my mother's father, who was the local ayurvedic doctor, or vaidhyan. He had an exceptional memory, otherwise he would not have been able to remember all the names of the herbs and potions he prescribed for his patients. I heard about how he had been apprenticed to the best vaidhyan in Varkala, the city where I had been born. It was all up to me, to study and learn and find out what I was good at.

I remember we had been digging up tapioca roots from the rocky soil. We had about a dozen covered in dark earth from the ground, and they had to be washed and peeled before being cut up for the cooking pot in the kitchen. It was late afternoon and I had been running around with my cousins all morning. I left my grandmother to clean the tapioca by the well, and then went to sleep on the cool floor where my sister lay in her hammock, slung from a beam on the ceiling. My cousins were still playing in the yard. Every now and again they would run in to swing the cradle. They were all excited for me, because my father was coming to visit us the following day. At just three years old, I had no idea who he was as I could not remember what he looked like. My grandmother was very happy to hear the news, and that was all that mattered to me.

The Consulting Rooms

We jostled for space near my grandfather's consulting room, leaning against the mahogany door frame, worn smooth by generations of children. Everyone said he was very old. He was nearly ninety, but patients still came to see him. He had been apprenticed to one of the most famous vaidhyans in the area at the beginning of his training in ayurveda at the turn of the twentieth century.

His consulting room was perched high on a cliff face. He had built his practice before the British had dug a railway line a few metres below his house, and ever since then, several times a day, trains had whistled to and from Thiruvananthapuram, the capital city of Kerala state. A railway station had been built not too far from his consulting rooms, and this had helped his reputation for restoring patients to health to grow far and wide over the years. Also as a result of the railways, his children had married further afield than anyone had imagined possible. He liked to grumble that although he admired the British for their enterprise and administrative skills, they had clouded his view with thick sooty smoke and their whistling trains often interrupted his consultations with noise pollution.

By the time I arrived on the scene, he'd had so many grandchildren he'd lost count. Giving us a cursory glance when we came to visit, he sometimes deigned to ask us who our mother was, just to make sure. Usually the patients answered discreetly on our behalf, indicating which of his daughters and sons had borne whom. We were too shy, too hesitant to do more than stare.

Around age five, I was fascinated by the scene. The small windows of his consulting room faced each other so there was a free current of air throughout the day. The doorway, also left open, led into a sunny walled-in yard which disappeared down some steep steps cut into the cliff-face, leaving just room enough on the rock ledge for each of us to walk up the steps one at a time. The furniture in the tiny consulting room was made of dark mahogany and the green concrete floor was always kept polished and clean. The whole area was off limits to us, so whenever we visited our grandfather we would cling to the smooth shiny door frame to take a look at the unfolding dramas. We huddled together, straining to hear of the numerous ailments that beset humanity. Psychological problems, physiological traumas, it didn't matter; the list was endless. But his patients always left with his stern advice and thick concoctions made on the premises, or a script to purchase herbal remedies from traditional vendors who lived on the opposite side of the railway lines.

He had always wanted to practise medicine, so as soon as he had been approved for his apprenticeship with the vaidhyan he had packed his bags and left the household for a few years. Meanwhile his child bride had remained in Edava with her family. They had grown up together, and when she attained puberty she had insisted on marrying him even though he was from a different social rank. He had far outshone any of her other suitors, she said. She had admired his strong supple body, his exuberance for life and his intelligence.

When they got married, she was twelve and he was twenty two. He had broad shoulders and a strong back, she said, and when they were small he used to piggyback her, even carrying her on his shoulders through the woodlands, as he looked for herbs to sell to the local medicine men. There were very few houses and plenty of virgin forest before the railways were laid down. He had been a wonderful young man, she said. If she had realised that the widowed daughter of his teacher would steal him from her, she would never have let him go away to study. She had not suspected at the time that he would soon become apprenticed to the older woman!

The woman had seduced him, my grandmother said, but that was life. However, she was proud of his many accomplishments. Both women were. He was a brilliant man and his children were all healthy and bright. They had nothing to complain about as he had a great knack for his chosen profession and was highly regarded by his community. Even so, when he returned with his mistress after completing his apprenticeship, my grandmother refused to cohabit. Many households had two wives living in the one home, she said, but she was having none of it. She had insisted on her independence. She had raised a storm at first and then held her ground.

That was the hardest thing she had ever done, she told me once, thinking back to far-gone days. Fortunately she hadn't succumbed to the pressure to conform even though many people had advised her to cohabit, as was the usual custom. She had remained determined in the face of all their scaremongering and she'd stood firm until the dust settled. After a period of uncertainty, things had changed. Once the women had set up their separate households, their relations began to improve. His new wife had settled within easy walking distance from my grandmother's home, so they were both able to see our grandfather. Over the ensuing years, what had started as an uneasy compromise blossomed into a healthy partnership. They learned to endure each other at a calculated distance, allowing their children to mingle amicably and run freely between the two households. Soon the two wives discovered that they had a great deal in common.

Both my grandmothers were beautiful, and part of my grandfather's success was due to their partnership, as they worked together to help him with his cures for patients needing special diets, often mixing the potions he prescribed. So by the time we came along, life had worked out for the best. We liked to trace our lineage by comparing our eyes, noses and toes. The genetic mix was a fascinating topic of conversation. Our different features came with interesting stories of romance and intrigue. It was an endless source of speculation finding out who had inherited what, as we worked out the creative facets of love's extraordinary handiwork.

I used to look at my grandfather in awe, wondering what I would look like when I grew old. His face was dark, strong and wrinkled. He hardly had any body weight on him. He followed a strict regime of exercise, a simple diet, and did not indulge in drink. People said my mother and I looked a little like him. Would I look like him in years to come, I wondered, staring at his dark round skull and the wrinkles lining his stern round-eyed face.

His breathing was calm and deliberate as he'd listen intently to his patients. There were long periods of silence interspersed by intense discourse. He spoke emphatically, asked questions and listened carefully. He rarely missed anything and insisted on clarifying statements and questions, always searching for gaps in meaning. He had learned over the decades, he said, that many people were reluctant to admit their sickness. They would pretend otherwise until they could ignore it no longer. After they'd left, sometimes all hell broke loose as he fumed over their ignorance and their appalling misdemeanours. He had known many of his patients all their lives. His reputation depended on getting the right information, but their ignorance and the secrets they kept from him was often his biggest problem. Apparently it wasn't an easy task to get them to admit the truth even if their lives were at stake.

'Habits,' he said, 'life-long habits. And they want me to fix them all up with a handful of herbs, roots and minerals. Then they are back again with a slightly different version of the same story, but it is usually the same problem. Some I have sent away never to come back. They can try some magician somewhere, if he is fool enough to take them on. Good luck and good riddance is what I say.'

He would seethe, deep in gloom, after such outbursts, especially if these patients were his lifelong friends. They were the ones who really tested his patience, whereas mostly it was an easy cavalcade of people who came and went. Word got around about his moods and his 'patients from hell'. It just added a special flavour to the consultation and people talked about some incidents for years. After a while they became part of our folklore.

Strange, I thought, that people should be so shabby with their own lives. Life was such a wondrous spectacle unfolding around me and I was impressed by the immensity which filled every nook and cranny. People flitted in and out of my vision, striking beings cocooned in their own special airs, moving against a background brimming with presence. Sounds, smells and sights combined as sensations as if swirling in a soup of life. How could they grow so weary about their lives and become so ignorant and petulant?

We would run out through the back door and climb onto a low wall to sit and watch the next train whistling past.

'The belly of the train has a huge furnace. You have to be careful not to get soot in your eyes, and if the soot sticks, don't rub your eyes with your fists. Let the tears run and you will see how they wash your eyes clean,' my cousins would advise, as we kept watch for a train, perched on the wall of the little yard, dangling our feet over the cliff face. My heart drummed in my chest in anticipation and I strained to hear the whistle blow, wondering from which direction the next train would come.

Later that evening we too would have to catch a train home. My mother only came down for day trips these days since she preferred to live in her own modern, red-tiled house in Mayyanad which my father had built for her before they were married.

I'd sit on a wooden plank in the second-class carriage of the train, loaded up with a bundle of herbs and medicines my grandmother had prepared to keep us healthy.

Land of Illusion

Our elder cousin was heading towards the paddy fields, his favourite hideout. We raced after him, running single file between the thorny bamboo fences separating the narrow side streets from people's yards. Annan was our leader, being a few years older. We admired the speed with which he ran, striving to catch up with him.

'They call this place Mayyanad, "the land of illusion". Can you believe that? What is the matter with the old folks? Have they lost their minds?' he called.

The paddy fields stretched as far as my eyes could see, ringed by tall palm trees. The water glistened in the vacant fields, reflecting the sunny blue sky, and white cranes trod lightly on the fields, pecking through the ripples made by their feet. The stream bubbled with foaming fresh water and our cousin pounced from pylon to pylon as he made his way across to the other side. Meanwhile we held back, cautiously straining to hear what he was saying about his recent escapade with the local policeman.

'He missed me every time,' Annan laughed as he gestured towards the fields. 'He was looking for a human being and not a lump of clay buried in the field!'

He had hidden here many times when he was a child, he said, burying himself deep in the clay soil. We huddled together, giggling at the thought, hoping to hear a little more about his plight. Lying low for ages, he had watched the frazzled policeman until he gave up the chase and wandered off to get a drink from the well nearby.

There were acres and acres of paddy fields on either side of the stream. We glanced at the well and then looked all around. What a clever manoeuvre, we thought, looking up at Annan with genuine admiration. It was a delight to hear his quick wit and see his confident smile. He did not take kindly to authority and had no hesitation in speaking his own mind.

This did not sit well with our elders, of course. Being an orphan, they said, he ought to know better and just do as he was told. He should consider himself lucky that everyone watched out for him.

'Why should I listen to the old folks?' he scoffed belligerently, looking down his nose at us in an exaggerated pose. 'They lie to your face. Look at this place, for heaven's sake. How can they call it an illusion?'

How strange, I thought, to call a place an illusion and then live in it for real. What a silly thing to say. Where did they draw the line between illusion and reality? As far as I could see, there was nothing unreal about the coconut groves, the small hamlets and the empty paddy fields. Even on a hot and sultry day like this, the fields looked substantial, set in the midst of a timeless rural landscape just waiting to be sown with rows upon rows of young green shoots once the rains had ceased.

'I think the old folks like to play with words because they have got nothing better to do,' our cousin continued. 'They call me all kinds of names. The trouble is that some of them stick, so don't believe everything they say about me.'

I listened with interest. To think we had spent so much time wondering about our own names. Feeling foolish, I looked over to the other side of the stream where a white crane was just about to take flight. Once in the air, it glided on an updraft and then swooped into a thicket where the pineapples grew, some distance away under the shade of tall coconut palms.

'That,' he said sternly pointing towards the thicket, 'is out of bounds. You had better stay on this side of the bank or I will feed you to the leeches.'

We nodded our heads assertively, mimicking him. That seemed fair enough. There was plenty of room on our side of the bank to play in the sand. So we clustered together in little groups to play our own games. We set about making mud pies, building hamlets, digging wells, tunnels and roads – working tirelessly through the afternoon. Not everything had a name, I reasoned with myself, creating numerous shapes in the sand with the dry husky fibrous coconut shells lying within my reach. When it came to real things like shells, wet sand and the giant white clouds floating in the sky, names really didn't matter, yet they existed anyway.

Years later, I would wonder what had become of my abiding sense of equanimity in the face of the numerous terms, the words we all used to figure things out. What had happened to my confidence in the underlying unity sustaining us all? Words, which had seemed like dispensable tools at first, gradually gathered a compelling force over time. Driven by a need to communicate, I soon began to take words more seriously. Too seriously. I immersed myself in words and was enthralled by my own imagination. Then I completely lost sight of unity, while I wrestled with my ideas of it instead. Like the frazzled policeman, I had looked and looked but could not see, since I was blinded by my vision of what I had sought.

Meanwhile the human being remained buried deep within me, watching and waiting for my eyes to clear so one day I would see that it is words that create illusions.

Learning from the Ground Up

Our daycare mother's name was Vasumati, derived from Vasana, meaning sweet perfume. We shortened it to Vashi, and then shortened it even more, calling her Shi-amma for fun because Vashi in Malayalam means wilful and she could be stubborn when we tried to make her bend the rules. She looked after me and my sister, along with her own son, during the day while my mother was teaching.

Shi-amma always dressed in white because she was a widow. She had a black and white photo of a very good-looking man in her front room, and said her husband had died young. From the photo, I could see that he had a regal bearing and wore a scarf around his neck. He was smiling in a refined and gentle manner at the camera when the shot was taken. She often glanced up at him as she hurried past the doorway, doing her work around the house and making sure that we did not run out onto the road. She had a three-room residence which was flanked by two verandahs, front and back – like many of the respectable houses in the area. The verandah overlooking the backyard led to a kitchen which had a roof tile made of clear glass to let in the sunlight. Not too far from the kitchen was a deep well with an open-air bathroom beside it. Near her kitchen was also a shed for storing firewood, coconut shells, baskets of ash and sawdust. The well was surrounded by a high fence made of woven palm fronds to give her privacy while she washed her clothes and bathed wearing a white sarong in the middle of the day, shortly after she had finished cooking for all of us.

Her house stood in the middle of a sand-covered yard which she swept clean every morning. In front of her house was a very tall mango tree which was famous in the area because the raw sour fruit was fabulous for making mouth-watering fish curries. Sometimes there were so many mangoes that fisher folk would come from their settlements near the Arabian Sea to buy them to sell in the local markets. Shi-amma also kept many hens which were overseen by a rooster from next door. Her hens were very clucky and laid lots of eggs in the pile of sawdust in the shed. She grew plenty of greens, pumpkins, bitter gourds and beans near the well. During the day she looked after my sister and me because our mother worked full-time as a teacher in a girls' high school across the paddy field, in a place which was famous for its many varieties of banana. Ever since her husband had died, Shi-amma had looked after children. She liked our company, and the extra income she earned helped with her household expenses. Even though her brother kept an eye out for her, she valued her own independence. Her brother lived closer to the markets, not too far from her family temple, which was called 'the pool of life'. He was well-educated and worked in the courts. If I studied hard, she said, there was no reason why I too could not be an advocate someday.

One day when I was about five, my mother asked Shi-amma to buy me a silver girdle for my waist, as I was about to begin my schooling. The girdle, to be worn against my bare skin, signified that I was growing up! Shi-amma said we would be passing her brother's house on the way to the market that day and she would introduce me to her family before we went on to a jeweller to buy the girdle. She said it was a good idea to have a girdle both for adornment and to give me strength to face all the challenges that were lying ahead in primary school.

Shi-amma's brother was tall and skinny, just like her. I looked up at him, noticing that he was wearing a white sarong and a fashionable blue nylon shirt, of a type made in Singapore. He said that my school was a good one and he was sure that I would do well there. Shi-amma explained that she would walk me past her old school on our way back from the gold and silver smith.

First came the fish market, where, from the street, I could hear the voices of many people haggling. But we did not go in so I could only try to imagine what the place was like. Next the jeweller's, some distance to walk from the market. The chubby jeweller was sitting on the floor beside a long glass case full of gold and silver jewellery. There were rings, bangles, chains and anklets in all sorts and designs. He looked me up and down while Shi-amma chose a girdle she liked, and then he reached for a measuring tape behind him. The glass case with all the jewels was lined in rich dark blue velvet. In the corner of the shop there was a small gas bottle, and the jeweller's apprentice was holding a long metal tube which had a blue flame spurting from it. The jeweller put the tape around my waist and grabbed a pen from behind his ear to scribble something on a pink notepad. He then put the pen back behind his ear and, looking down his nose at me, raised his eyebrows and asked if I could read and write.

I shook my head with a look of aversion.

'The sooner you learn to read and write, the better,' he said, looking at Shi-amma admonishingly. 'The girdle alone will not do the trick, Sweet Perfume. You should get her older siblings to teach her if you can't be bothered!'

'You always have an opinion about everything that is of no concern to you!' grumbled my daycare mother.

I looked at them both with interest. There was always so much drama when the elders got together.

'Remember how we used to scratch around writing in the sand with bamboo sticks to learn our alphabets?' asked the goldsmith. They had both been to the school at White Sands, I gathered from their conversation. I would be going to a private school which was in Andhra Pradesh. They even knew of Krishnamurti, the founder of the special school, because they had heard about him from my parents when my father first went to work for him at the school. As the two chatted about old times, the goldsmith cut the length of silver chain Shi-amma had chosen and gave it to his apprentice, muttering some instructions in an aside to him. The young boy quickly turned on the blue flame and with great dexterity set about attaching a hook and a decorative leaf onto each end of my chain. He then wrapped it in pink transparent paper and gave it to Shi-amma. She carefully took some notes out of her purse and paid the goldsmith, while asking him to make sure he wrote out a receipt for my mother. She was going to take me to her family temple so the priest could bless a charm to hang from my girdle, she said.

Shi-amma's family temple was close to the railway station, and surrounded by high walls. She told me there was a large pool inside, and on auspicious occasions she would come down with her extended family and they would all bathe to cleanse themselves before making offerings to the gods. The pool was full of dark water and there were rows of steps going down to it. It was surrounded by large rain trees covered in pink powder-puff blooms which were laced with cream pollen. I saw a group of children splashing in the pool, which was an unexpected sight because there were no pools we were allowed to swim in near our home. Seeing me look eagerly at the children, Shi-amma said she would go to the priest on my behalf so I too could play by the pool. Some of the children recognised me. They were racing around naked among the trees and I noticed that many of them wore girdles. I could see that some of the children had already been blessed because they had streaks of sandalwood paste across their foreheads. The sandalwood would keep the brain from overheating, they were told. Many said they were already learning to read and write.

I thought about the few lessons we had had over the past weeks. Each evening while the women gathered to talk over the fence, our older siblings would call out to us to gather by the gate. There were about six of us beginning school in the new year. To start our lessons, one of us had to sweep the long wide path from the fence post to the front steps leading to the verandah. Then my adolescent cousin Usha would write the Malayalam alphabet on the sand with a long bamboo stick. When she was done, she would call out to our older cousin and he would suddenly appear at the gate, grab a long bamboo stick and take over.

'Look to the ground! Cover your eyes! Say the word! Underscore!' he would repeat loudly, herding us towards each symbol on the sand and pointing to it imperiously. We hung back in hesitation, taking turns to say each word that he pointed to with the bamboo stick. When I looked at the symbol upside down, he would grab me by the shoulder and stand me in front of the squiggle so I was looking at it the right way up. I stared as hard as I could at what looked like the shape of a caterpillar to me.

'Now cover your eyes!' my cousin ordered, and I slapped my palms firmly over my eyeballs, watching in surprise as an array of red and blue colours gathered behind my eyelids.

'Say the word, "Ah!"' ordered my cousin, from behind me.

'Ah!' I said, obliging him. I then waited while the others took turns to repeat the sound after me. We were learning to recognise the symbols so that we could read them from a book later on. When he was satisfied that we had said each sound correctly, he would say, 'Mm ... underscore!' We'd all sigh and grin with relief at each other, huddling back together to read the next symbol.

We moved along from the fence post to the verandah in the shade of the sour mango tree, jumping backwards every time we pronounced a symbol right.

'Thara, mara, para, vara,' our older siblings called out, making sure we went about the repetitive business of memorising each symbol one by one.

Shi-amma would make sure we carried out this routine half a dozen times and then she would show us the new symbol for the following day. She would draw it out on a fresh patch of earth at the base of the mango tree where no one was likely to step on it. The symbols had to be memorised each day, my cousins told us loftily, until they stuck like glue in our mind's eye.

They said that somewhere inside my head there was a 'third eye' which would oversee everything I learned off by heart. So I had to be very careful to pay full attention to make sure that I got it right each time. Shutting my eyes tight, I looked and looked to find where this third eye was. I could feel my eyes crossing over with the intensity of my inward gaze. So many years later, I can see that a lot of that sounding out has stuck, though whether due to my 'third eye' or not, I still don't know.

As we walked past Shi-amma's school in White Sands, she told me she really liked my silver girdle because it was heavy and ornate. Like gold, silver has a good resonance, she explained, and wearing it around my hip would keep me well and truly grounded so I would not float away with the fairies, getting caught up in too many fantasies which would surely confuse my mind.

A Rose by any other Name

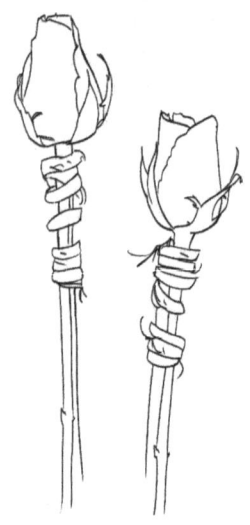

'Stay off the roses!' roared Reddy, the head gardener of Rishi Valley School in Andhra Pradesh. 'They are full of sharp thorns that will prick you if you are not careful.'

Keeping our distance, we watched as he lifted two heavy tin cans full of water slung from a pole across his shoulders and made his way through the cluster of rose bushes in his garden. He looked rather funny because his gait was exaggerated and his neck leaned forward under the strain of balancing the load. Soon after moving to the school when I was six, I realised that the garden was his pride and joy. He spent hours tending it so it would remain a feast of colour all year round.

He said that there were varieties of roses that no one had ever seen before in the ancient valley which had been his home from birth. There was even a 'blue rose,' he said, pausing to see if we were impressed. We looked impressed on cue, so as not to disappoint him. The rose itself was an indifferent colour of blue but the conversation was getting interesting and we stayed on. In the early days when he yelled at us we would scramble off in a hurry, not knowing what was amiss. Then, gradually, he began to trust us so we lingered. We weren't going to trample on his roses, he realised. We were just a bunch of junior school kids more interested in what he was doing than his roses.

Every now and then when we encountered him at the water tank, he would give us snippets of information about what was blooming in his garden. There were marigolds, jacarandas, jasmine, zinnias and a host of other flowers with unpronounceable names. Bougainvilleas, oleanders ... the list just kept on tripping off his tongue.

'Oh, my!' I thought. 'What a lot of difficult names to learn.'

He liked to rattle off these English words with some deliberation and a special twist of relish. They were his domain after all. He had been working in the gardens all his life and there was plenty to show for it.

Genuinely impressed by his garden, we also admired his eloquence. We all knew that English was a very important language. We looked at his flowers afresh, seeing for the first time how different they were. Until then we had just thought of them as flowers. It seemed that each one had an exclusive name, and a different colour and way of seeding at the end of the season. The world was becoming an intricately bewildering place the more we learned about it. Most of us were not well versed in English and had learned to compromise with smiles, nods, nudges and gestures to get the message across as we played together. Listening to him reel off the botanical names of plants made us realise that we still had a long way to go.

We spoke about five Indian languages between us, but since Sanskrit is the root of all South Indian languages, we managed to communicate reasonably well. English was our common language, just as the British had wanted it to be, we were told. Learning at an 'English medium school' set us apart from the general population of students, who attended state-funded schools where the local language was given priority. However, there was a general consensus among Indians that although the British had been unceremoniously kicked out in the 1940s, they had left behind a legacy that was not entirely unwelcome. English equalled progress, we were told. There was no doubt about that. The world was opening up to an independent India and English was an important bridge to make the transition from the atrocious tyranny of British rule to the remarkable age of science which would set the scene for the twenty-first century.

The garden around the auditorium was especially important, Reddy assured us. It was the very centre of the school, where scholars, scientists, politicians and international visitors met with the remarkable teacher, Krishnamurti, to discuss the plight of the world, in the hope of finding a solution to the interminable problems in human relationships and, it was hoped, bring about peace on earth.

'Roses are highly regarded around the world. That's why we have so many of them in this garden, and I've lost count of the number of people who have admired these flowers year after year,' Reddy boasted.

'Some visitors bring special varieties for me to plant here. That's how this garden has grown from a few bushes when I came to work as a young man, to now this!'

He looked around with pride as we looked at his roses again. They had merely been green, prickly bushes with a few bright flowers until then. We had even planned, when we were in kindergarten, to pick the red pointy buds and use them as spear heads for our mock battles. By tying them onto thin bamboo poles, we could thrust these at each other to show off our combat skills. Now suddenly that did not seem like a good idea.

The blooms stood out once I paid attention, whereas until then, all their subtle colours and different shades had passed me by unnoticed, I realised. Now we marvelled at them as he pointed affectionately to one and then another, taking care to tell us their names in both English and Telugu.

'Smell them if you wish, but take care not to break them. They are most beautiful flowers. In English folklore, they are a symbol of love. Here in India we sing about their beauty and smell. Sniff them and the sweet perfume will surely fill your heart.'

We sniffed the perfume in wonder and looked at each other, our eyes bulging with delight as we inhaled deeply. Our noses twitched as we exhaled together noisily.

'Haaa!' we exclaimed.

Reddy laughed at our surprise, his dark lanky body shaking with suppressed mirth. I could see that he was surprised by our reaction. He hadn't expected us to be so forthright in our delight. Walking past the bushes that were shoulder high, we smiled at him differently. The 'spear heads' had completely vanished from our minds as we looked at his roses with enormous respect.

We hadn't suspected that so much work went into tending the garden. On numerous occasions, we had randomly run over it in search of butterflies, earth worms and a variety of garden bugs. None of us had realised that the perfume wrapped in those petals was the same the world over. Here right in our midst was a 'world secret' that we had completely overlooked. I was full of admiration.

As I walked towards the playgrounds, I began to feel a different sense of purpose in my stride. The landscape had suddenly changed for me. This whole place was intimately connected to the rest of the world and I was privileged to be a part of it. I felt there was a lot to learn about the world, so much still to discover.

Beloved of the Gods

'Thought is limited,' my teacher told me when I was about six years old.

'So what?' I thought. 'I can think endlessly!'

'Knowledge is limited,' he said. 'What's the big deal?' I thought. 'I can learn endlessly!'

Having sorted out my concerns for the time being, I sauntered off to the hills where the sweet custard apples grew. If I was lucky, I thought, I might find a ripe one in the bush before the birds or mice got to it.

Looking down at my feet, I realised that I had forgotten to put on my slippers, but that didn't matter. I only wore them out of courtesy to the finer sensitivities of the residential school community at Rishi Valley. Slippers were a status symbol. For some reason you had to remove them as a mark of respect to someone greater than you. But the local folk did not have to worry about such things because they walked barefoot. They couldn't afford slippers. They were extremely poor and humble, and I had begun to love them, so I didn't want to pretend that I was greater than them by leaving my slippers on all the time.

I lived in Andhra Pradesh with my father while my mother stayed on in Kerala to teach in high school. Our house was near a mango grove on the outskirts of the school property. The lady who took care of me during the day came from the first village called Poojarivari Palli. Her name was Papul Amma. She had been widowed and was raising her three children – two girls and a boy – on her own, and she was happy to have a job at our place. Her two youngest children were close to my age so she let us all play together.

'I have managed to bring up my children on my own,' she said to me. 'One more will not make a big difference.'

I felt very grateful to be accepted into the fold. Like my lovely grandmother whom I had left behind in Kerala, Papul Amma had a toothless smile. Because of this, I was drawn to her instantly even though we didn't speak the same language. She was employed to do chores around the house, fetch our meals from the school dining hall, comb my hair in the mornings and make sure I wore clean clothes every day.

Once a week I had an oil bath with her two younger children, Jayamma and Venkatramana. She rubbed us over from head to toe, making sure that our bodies were covered with slithery brown jinjili, an oil made from ground nuts, our word for peanuts. Then she gave me a vigorous rubdown while we were waiting for the water to heat up in a copper urn built into the corner of the bathing room. For bathing, we'd be lathered and sluiced using cups of warm water. As we huddled waiting by the door, we fed kindling into the fire she lit, making sure we kept it going until the water was close to boiling.

There were plenty of dry twigs and cut wood to be salvaged from the mango grove, which spread out over a few acres behind the house. Papul Amma usually stacked a pile of wood outside under the stairs, and before our bath we would scramble about the great backyard, gathering dry twigs to restock the pile. She wouldn't let us go under the stairs for fear of snakes, scorpions and millipedes which sheltered in the woodpile. The stairs led to the rooftop, so once the fire had died out and the chimney had stopped smoking, we would climb the stairs to play on the terrace or sit up there under the stars until my father returned from work late in the evening.

While playing with her children, I soon I began to learn Telugu, the main language along with English that was spoken at school. I spoke Malayalam with my father and Tamil with some other friends. To my surprise, I discovered that I had a real interest in languages.

Papul Amma told me that Krishnamurti was from a nearby town called Madanapalle. He was a beautiful man, surely a beloved of the gods, she said. He had wandered all over the world in search of truth and had returned to settle his scores with the gods near his birthplace. He had turned the bare brown earth into a fertile landscape and built a great place of learning where people came from all over the world to listen to him and watch him teach the children of his school how to enquire into the human condition. He had brought prosperity to his people and created a way of life that few had imagined possible.

'You are lucky to study here,' Papul Amma said. 'You must listen very carefully to everything that is being said.'

'Where do the gods live?' I asked quickly, not wishing to miss any key points she was making as she tugged away at my hair to help unleash its knots.

'They have withdrawn from us because of our conduct. Now they live in the hills so they can keep an eye on us from a distance. If you look at how the sun sets over Rishi Konda, you will understand why they chose those hills. From there they can see the world and watch the clouds gather the sun each day, turning it into a molten ball of gold. From there, they can watch over us.'

Fascinated, I listened to her voice through the sound of the comb raking along my skull, my head dipped, waiting for her to finish plaiting my long black hair. My eyes were stinging from the pain of the wide-toothed plastic comb. She wiped the comb on her hips and reached for some ribbons tucked into her waistline to tie my plaits. When the task was done, she held me at arm's length to examine her handiwork. Satisfied, she let me go. We exchanged a smile and I raced out the front door, leaving my slippers behind. Breathing deeply, I was relieved that she'd decided I'd turned out alright.

I was free to do as I pleased on Sundays as long as I returned home for lunch. I glanced at the hills that rose high around the valley. It felt as if the earth was holding us in the palm of her hand. I loved the blue of the sky and the clouds that floated languidly by. The sky was a different blue to the hills that etched the horizon to the east and west. Some days the lines between the sky and the hills mingled in the heat haze of high noon, and then distinguished themselves again in the ever-changing light, as clouds sailed across the sky. Both the vast expanse of sky curving over the valley and the strange granite boulders that were strewn around the landscape filled me with a sense of awe and wonder. The sheer mass of the hills looming over the landscape had a profound impact on my mind.

How could I take in so much at a glance, I wondered, as my view fell to the ground. The track that led into the hills had worn down to a fine dust in places as it meandered around boulders too big for human hands to shift.

My father said that men had fought two world wars and dropped an atom bomb on Japan, but the valley had endured all and gone on with the greater business of nurturing and sustaining life. When the war started he had been a young man in Sri Lanka. He had enlisted to join the army but he had been rejected due to his poor eyesight. In despair, he had bought a Bhaghavad Gita, the sacred text, and had set out to learn it all off by heart in case he lost his eyesight. Later he heard that an Englishman called Gordon Pearce was interviewing people to help the teacher, Krishnamurti, establish a school in a remote region of India called Andhra Pradesh. So my father applied, and started working in the estates of the fledgling school. He fancied himself as a resident nurse and liked to help the locals when they were sick.

I knew that during his youth he had helped out in the dispensary at St Thomas College in Gurutalava. He would have loved to become a doctor but never had the opportunity, he told me. After his mother had died in a cyclone when he was seven, his father had taken him to Ceylon where he worked as a houseboy for well-to-do families until he later worked for Rollo and Mary Hayman who ran a college in Gurutalava. They had taught him to read, write and speak correct English.

When he first came to the valley, he said it had felt as if the rest of the world had ceased to exist. He had gladly left behind the wars, the religious riots and the intense feelings of hatred cultivated by different groups of people with their infernal distrust and mindless greed. The valley lived and breathed serenely through all this chaos; granite boulders soaked up the sunshine in the midst of an arid, dreamy wilderness. The school had grown from nothing, he explained, pointing to a few ancient footpaths that had criss-crossed the valley for centuries. He loved hiking all over the place on these paths with his colleagues. On excursions into the jungles in Ceylon, he would often come upon ancient monuments in the jungle. The temple at the foot of the Rishi Konda hills was thought to be thousands of years old.

'That is a long, long time!' he emphasised, and his face grew sombre as he deliberated over the span of time.

I watched a dragonfly land precisely on a yellow bloom which was blowing in the wind. Its transparent wings sparkled in the clear sunlight as it struggled to tuck them securely to its side. As its bulging eyes misted over, I watched rainbow colours float over the clear film of its eyeballs. Then it spread its wings, rose above the bloom and suddenly vanished from my sight.

Thousands of years, I thought. I could not make out what he meant.

Up in the hills, some of the ancient tracks were wedged deep into the ground. I loved to walk on these tracks that meandered through the hills along the loops and hollows which were carved out to suit the lie of the land. They hadn't changed for thousands of years, even though hundreds of people walked over them each year.

As I struggled in my mind to gain some understanding of the stretch of time, I wondered again about Krishnamurti's concern that our thoughts and knowledge are so limited.

I felt grand as I strode along, making sure I was striking the hard surface of the path with my heels first, rather than mincing around on my tippy-toes. I looked down and saw my feet covered in fine soft dust from thousands of years past.

The Sandalwood Tree

I was about six, standing alone under the sandalwood tree near the verandah of my home in Rishi Valley, Andhra Pradesh. My mother and sister had gone back to Kerala the day before and I was wondering when I would see them again. Amma had told me that the red sandalwood tree had special medicinal properties and her father used it in Ayurvedic medicine to treat a wide range of health issues such as heart disease, digestive problems and acne. So in my heart the tree had a magical reputation, and standing under its cool shade always made me feel happy.

An old English couple who lived next door, about thirty metres from our place, were walking towards their house. My mother had introduced me to Harry and Hilda Moorhead recently when she went over to say goodbye before going home to Kerala. Harry helped with the estates and Hilda assisted in running the junior school. They had been interested in Krishnamurti's aim to establish a school and had helped to get it under way.

As they greeted me, I waved at them shyly. I had never seen white folk until I came to the valley, and had at first studied them inquisitively, hiding behind my mother's sari. Harry had been a soldier and had faced great physical and emotional suffering during the war, my father said, making a grimace as he thought about such pain and horror. Hilda was always dressed in pale floral dresses which came down to her knees, and she wore soft silk scarves round her curly grey hair. She had a kind smile which made my heart race, and she was admired for her capable authority. She was always smiling at their dog called Browny who would come bounding out to greet them.

I had been uncertain about dogs ever since one had snarled and chased me round the yard at my home in Kerala when I was just a toddler. Unlike the strays which were nervous as they yelped and bayed during the rutting season, Browny looked amicable and docile, and he wagged his tail an awful lot. The Moorheads were good friends of my father, since they all worked on the estates which belonged to the school. They would often talk animatedly together about some project or other.

Framing the entrance to their house was a wonderful bougainvillea weighed down with crimson flowers, and their garden was well-maintained by a happy young gardener called Dustagiri.

Standing with my parents while my mother said goodbye, I had looked at Hilda's fine leather shoes, her purse and her freckled white skin beneath her dress, and listened to their conversation. As they spoke of things that did not concern me, there was little that I could understand, not even why she wore shoes. By contrast, Browny and I were truly engaged. We were at eye level with each other. As well as wagging his tail, he smiled and panted.

'Perhaps she can keep a diary each day to describe her life and then one day we can discover what goes on in the mind while growing up,' I had heard Hilda say to my father, my 'Cha', with laughter in her voice.

I had looked up at them in astonishment. They had to be joking! How could I possibly capture all that was going on in words? There simply weren't enough words. More work for me, I sulked. I hated the squiggles I made in the work books every day. Learning to write Malayalam was hard enough, and then during the past year, I had gone over the whole process again in learning to write English. I bristled with resentment, while joyful Browny wagged at me, inviting me to go for a run.

Things are not joyful, I felt like saying to him. There was a conspiracy afoot, unfolding right over our heads. Slowly I heard the jocular tone of their conversation subside. I looked at my father to check if he was serious. He was fully engaged in the conversation, smiling and nodding as they all deliberated together. Shifting from one foot to another, I looked on with a sense of gloom. Would I ever learn enough words in English to describe what went on in my mind, I wondered? There were so many words that I had not heard before and most of the time my understanding was patchy. Lately I kept stumbling over a burning desire to keep up with adult conversations. Trust the old folk to think up something like this. I wished they would take their plans elsewhere because I was having enough trouble trying to comprehend what was going on as it was.

The conversation ended with genial laughter just as we heard the sound of a bullock cart turn the corner. It was coming up a road that was lined with large agave with leaves each about a meter long. Each succulent leaf ended in a long sharp thorn the colour of polished mahogany. On hearing the sound of wheels, I took Browny's hint and ran towards home, thrilled to be able to race him and catch up with him. He was not a bad dog, after all. What's more, he was honest and frank, and he ran whenever it suited him. I wish I was a dog, I thought. I wouldn't have to do homework and could scamper about, sniffing around the valley all day.

I don't fancy being a bullock, though, I thought, as I cast my eyes over the yard. Those animals worked really hard. Cha said the young bullocks were picked early in life and had to be gradually trained to carry heavy loads. I had seen them carry huge columns of granite for the building work that went on around the school. I'd been astonished by their incredible strength.

The bullocks came into view, plodding with passive resignation and barely casting a glance at the road, while the driver sat on the mid-beam, flicking his whip this way and that, clicking his tongue, and pulling on the bridle. He was relaxed and entirely in control of his animals as they wore large metal rings through their moist black noses. Their doe-like eyes were pools of darkness surrounded by long black eyelashes. They rarely looked me in the eye but seemed entirely bent on getting somewhere. The ropes told them where to go because they were very sensitive to the pull of the ring on their noses. They probably just plodded along to avoid the threat of pain. At least they didn't have to do pages and pages of copy writing, I thought, my mind filling with envy once again at the thought of their lifestyle. The rider was a good man, Cha said, and he was impressive to look at in more ways than one. He had a strong straight back as he sat proudly on his cart with a posture not unlike Krishnamurti's. A dark, lean, wiry and tall man, he had long black hair that he tied in a knot on the top of his crown. He put on a great balancing act as he guided the animals along the dirt roads in the valley. He would call them by name and show his care for them by keeping them clean and well-fed.

The cart was hand-made, 'a masterpiece of craftsmanship,' I would hear the elders comment as they stood around conversing. The wood had been sourced specially for the vehicle, which had extra large wheels to travel great distances for years. The wheels were lined in cast iron and the wooden spokes were wedged securely into the curved frames. The animals must be paired correctly to work well together, my father had explained to me once. These animals were the best pair that he had come across. The cart was balanced in such a way that when the animals stopped, the wheels took the pressure off their shoulders, so easing their burden. I marvelled at the engineering that went into such craftsmanship.

I admired the bullock cart so much that I decided that one day I would buy one and ride it the way he did. I had heard of jet engines and planes but I had not seen any of them at close hand. Besides, a cart would suit the lie of the land very well. The dirt roads around our house were made for it and I loved the thought of a vehicle that was hand-made from special wood that would last a lifetime. I had seen pictures of gods riding chariots through the clouds. I would paint my cart in gold, tie my hair in a knot and lord it over my animals all day long.

I didn't like horses, though. Not so long ago in Madanapalle, one had neighed impatiently in my ear while stamping its feet and champing at the bit. They also wore special eye pads to keep them on the straight and narrow. Otherwise they tended to become restless, or might 'freeze', refusing to move. I didn't fancy the life of a donkey either, I thought, as I watched Browny sniffing manure by the rose bush. They carried huge loads and were bullied by people. And they brayed, grunted and bared their teeth ever so inelegantly. A black ant was scouting around the path by my feet, holding its backside up with ferocious determination. One had to be watchful in the garden as there were plenty of creepy-crawlies everywhere. The ants were especially fierce and became really annoyed when they were stepped on. Ants got to travel through tunnels underground, though. I wondered what that would be like, to spend my life underground carrying earth and food and waving at my mates with long tentacles to pick up on the latest news.

Focusing on the conversation again, I recalled Uma, a young woman who had taught me to write back home in Kerala. She had been a disciplinarian. She 'produced results,' Amma had told me when she sent me to her to learn to write. Then, when I'd first come to the Krishnamurti school here in Andhra Pradesh a year ago, I had been afraid the teachers would rap my knuckles with a ruler if I did not write well. But my new teacher, an Australian called Maureen Flanagan, had been patient and kind. Unfortunately, having spent money on tuition for me to write in

Malayalam, my mother insisted that I also do a page of Malayalam writing each day after classes at my English medium school. Malayalam, she insisted, created a different mind because it had so many Sanskrit words. Seeing no way out, I persevered with glum determination by spending an hour each evening, clutching my left hand under my right armpit while I learned to write with my right hand. 'Reading, riting and rithmetic, the three Rs,' my father often said, rolling out his Rs as he coaxed me to finish a page each day. He knew as well as I did that my mother would check on us when we visited her in Mayyanad during vacation.

I slouched over the desk, slavishly tracing the curly letters in Malayalam while other thoughts flitted through my mind. I caught myself imagining bullock carts with gold wheels flying through some marvellous clouds floating in the sky. Cha would sit flapping his newspaper as he read avidly page after page while the radio played Indian melodies softly in the background. Every now and then he would look at me over his reading glasses and assure me, 'Where there's a will there's a way!'

Apparently all this effort was going to help me to live a good life. I had no idea how that could be. The good life for me was to run around the valley and hike around the hills, watch people go about their daily lives and stand under the sandalwood tree. That vast valley was an extraordinary place, and since there were no walls and boundaries to keep any person out, there was a feast of activity going on every day just waiting to be discovered.

Time moved on ... whether I practised my writing or not. Soon I saw that the elderly couple who had been wandering about admiring their garden had already disappeared into their stone cottage built of grey granite carved from the surrounding hills. And the shade of the sandalwood tree had also moved away from me, I realised, as I emerged from my reverie.

A Common Well

I was walking beside Papul Amma, my daycare mother or 'Ayah'. She wore some charms around her neck which were made from silver. She said some of the symbols had special powers.

'God only knows what they mean. I can't read, but my mother consulted the local priest and he said these charms would keep me safe from evil,' she told me.

I looked at the symbols drawn on the circular charms which were threaded through a black chord interspersed with several blue, yellow, red and green beads around her neck. They were a feast of colours against her dark skin. She also had red, green and gold glass bangles round her wrists. Dressed in a yellow blouse and maroon sari which had a yellow border to match her blouse, she had an embroidered green and maroon pouch tucked into her hip over her sari. The pouch was decorated with mirror-work embroidery and contained her personal care items and her betel leaves, which were a luxury she could afford.

She took me by the hand and we hurried along the dusty road together. She was going to take me to her village to introduce me to her folk. I could play with the children in the village without spending the whole afternoon with my head buried in a fat book, she said. She was talking about Grimm's Fairy Tales that our neighbours, Mr and Mrs Moorhead, had given me as a gift for my sixth birthday early in the year.

'Children your age should not spend so much time reading like that. Childhood is such a precious time and there is so much more to life than imagining all kinds of wild things!' Papul Amma would tell me.

I had been reading about giants and fairies and had often tried to regale her with the stories of Rapunzel and Jack and the beanstalk, but unlike me, she was not very impressed by any of them. They were unsuitable for children my age she said, looking disdainfully at the book. She wouldn't be at all surprised if I had bad dreams with such stories teeming through my mind. As I walked along with her, I thought it over and had to agree that the stories seemed rather bizarre compared to the pastoral setting of the newly tilled farmlands that we were heading towards.

'Many of the fields are bare, but the dark green ones here and there are covered in ground nuts,' Papul Amma pointed out, her bangles tinkling as she indicated with a graceful gesture the dark green fields alongside the dry gully which cut through the valley.

The road we were walking on had a groove on either side where the bullock cart wheels had turned the sand to a fine dust over hundreds of years. Our path was covered in a myriad of footprints.

'Those are mine from this morning,' she said, pointing to the set of footprints that headed towards my home. 'I can see there hasn't been much traffic through here today. Some days all you see are the footprints of goats and cattle.'

After that, I looked out for her footprints all the way to the village. We made a game of finding them as we walked on towards the east, about a kilometre beyond the school grounds. Sometimes she would point to the footprints of people she recognised and tell me stories of the folk who walked along the dirt road regularly. They were all from the same village, she said. They had all grown up together and now many of them worked at the school. Some people further up the track worked in the town, which was sixteen kilometres away by bus. Most of the villagers tended to fields that had been in their families for generations.

Every now and then we came across large tamarind trees beside the road where we could stop and shelter from the direct rays of the sun. As we came up to one, Papul Amma confided to me, 'The price of tamarind has gone up. Who would have thought that there would be an income in these? When we were little we only valued them for their shade. Now once a year when the crop is ready, a man from the town comes here and pays money for the fruit. He and his family make a living picking, drying and curing the fruit to sell in the big cities.'

I looked in awe at the large gnarled brown branches of the tree. I knew what food she was referring to but I couldn't see how such a beautiful tree could produce the black gooey substance that was an essential ingredient in many curries. I looked at the tree with renewed respect, knowing what a difference its fruit could make to a dish.

What a tremendous tree, I thought, to provide so much shade and so much food for so many people across the country. I loved the dark brown colour of the craggy bark which covered the trunk. It stood out in sharp contrast to the light green feathery leaves which completely covered its branches. The massive limbs scaled the heights, tapering to a pinnacle which was hidden from my view. So impressed, I stood by the trunk, looking up with my head thrown back as far as it could go, while Papul Amma cooled off in the shade of the tree which covered the road and part of a field.

She unwound her dark curly hair and shook her head to let the air cool her scalp. Then she ran her fingers through her hair and massaged the back of her neck before tying her hair in a knot again. We sat in the dust for a while looking at the evidence of others who had taken shelter there. Around the large round trunk there were several used matchsticks, a few unused scraps of nicotine leaves and a rusty old red tin without a lid that someone had left behind.

'As we get closer to the village there will be stray dogs and cattle, so keep close to me,' she warned. 'They're afraid of me because I won't take any nonsense from them. If they bite you, you can become very sick, so it's important to keep your distance.'

I heard the note of caution in her voice and remembered the mating season of the dogs back in Kerala when for days the packs ran wild, the dogs baying, yapping and snarling all night long. We were never allowed to go out unsupervised during that season and one of our older cousins was always in command during those times.

I took Papul Amma's hand immediately and stayed close to her, feeling her feet quicken as we got closer to her home. I looked eagerly about me. We were turning the loop of a winding road so I could not see what was on the other side. Once past the tall cactuses that lined the road, I looked over a vast expanse of flat land with a village of red mud huts closeted in a circle at the foot of a green hill covered in granite boulders. It was like nothing I had ever seen before. The huts were of rammed red earth and the roofs were made of thick, packed yellow straw to keep the heat out. The doorways were small and beautifully decorated with a string of mango leaves across the front. There were also ornate symbols drawn in white flour in the tiny front yard of each hut. The design or kolam, made up of curving lines and circles, was similar to those Papul Amma drew daily outside our yard. As we looked at each other, we smiled and our eyes spoke volumes. At last I would get to see where she lived.

'You can choose the symbol for today and I will show you how to draw one in my yard,' she agreed, reading my train of thought and understanding my fascination.

Her yard was of beaten earth plastered over with cow dung. It had been swept clean in the morning by her elder daughter. She opened her little wooden door, which was painted blue, and looked inside to check if there was water in the earthenware pot. As we drank some, she said I should stay inside while she went out in search of her children. They were probably playing in the fields with others, she explained.

Soon the word spread that she was back in the village and her children had returned with her. They offered to take me back to play with them. We ran out together to the fields while she stayed behind to cook their meal for the night. The fields had been weeded, raked and tilled, so we were safe from snakes. Because it was so dry in this part of the country, the fields were only fit to grow millet or sugar cane, I learned. There was a common well in the middle of the village where everyone could draw water. This was strange to me because back in Kerala most families had their own wells.

The children led me to this important place and we looked over the low wall at the reflections deep inside the well. We children laughed at each other, pulling faces and gesticulating. Others came out to look at me because many of them knew my father who managed the dairy farm for our school. They were talking among themselves because the school farm employed many families in the village.

They smiled and said how long my hair was and told me that I had lovely eyes. I thought they were all beautiful but I did not speak their language well enough to be able to tell them so. We all smiled instead and made do running up and down little alleyways, chasing goats and cats and jumping over chickens which cackled as we came at them. There were women issuing warnings and children squealing with laughter.

It was getting late and in the distance a boy yodelled to warn us that the goats were returning from the hills. Cows stood lamely by their houses chewing cud as if mesmerised by the timeless enchantment of the place. I could see that the shadows were lengthening as the sun began to dip behind the blue hills far off in the distance. I noticed that there was not a cloud in the sky as I heard my name being called out urgently by someone.

Papul Amma was looking for me. If I hurried down the road, we could hitch a ride from a friend who'd offered to take us back in his bullock cart so we'd get back before dark. Reluctantly, I left the beloved place in time to catch the ride back home as the sun set.

I don't want to be alone with my book again, I thought with a feeling of disdain. Nothing I had read about villages in the fairy tales had prepared me for the fun I'd had with the village children. And we did not even speak the same language, I realised. We were living in such different worlds and yet we had so much in common in the here and now.

Salute

There were cobras in the valley, green snakes and bats. There were scorpions, centipedes, millipedes and wasps. As I thought of these creatures I felt my shoulders tense, and noticed that I hadn't included the butterflies, dragonflies, blue jays, parrots, weaver birds and kites which flew about in the sky. There were also mosquitoes which were bloodsuckers, I continued thinking dolefully. They flocked around, serenading me in the evenings with a high-pitched note, and only stopped when they took a drink of my blood through their long needling snouts. Sitting on the front doorstep outside the verandah, I heaved a sigh, unable to ward off a sense of inertia flooding through my mind. I couldn't for the life of me figure out what to do, being on my own.

The circular lawn in front of the house had a flowering bougainvillea which was over three metres tall. The white and pink flowers trailed over a margosa tree that stood at the centre of the lawn. Near the front verandah stood a sandalwood tree which had grown of its own accord. Underneath was another bougainvillea which refused to flower because it was too much in the shade, according to my father. When my sister Girija and my cousin Jayan had visited, we had turned that shady space into a cubby house by hanging a worn red sheet between the branches to act as a roof. A terracotta teapot with a dragon motif on it, broken bits of china from the back of the house, tins of Bournvita, Horlicks bottles and soda bottles were still in their places, beckoning invitingly. But I did not wish to play alone for fear of encountering snakes and scorpions.

It was mid-afternoon. The sun was pouring down from a clear blue sky and the half moon was barely visible in the light of day. None of the stars that I saw at night could be seen but they were still there, I realised. I just had to wait a few more hours to see an entirely different kind of display. The world was a magical place full of mystery and yet I did not really want to go exploring it on my own.

Seeing me sitting by myself, my father went back in through the front door and came out with a list of items to pick up from the tuck shop, which was some distance away. He had run out of a few staples at the farm, he said. They needed Dettol antiseptic and Vaseline petroleum jelly for the cows. If I could get them from Captain Nair, who was in charge of the store, my father could take a little nap. It would save him a long walk and he could go straight back to work on my return from the shop.

'I've included Cadbury's chocolate in the list,' he said in encouragement. 'You can have a piece for afternoon tea.' Suddenly I felt a quickening of interest and was a little overcome by a sense of greed. I decided that I liked Captain Nair because he spoke Malayalam and had a large moustache of grey curly hair, which made him look ferocious. The list in my hand, I ran down the footpath, cutting across the circular lawn and through the bush towards the eastern part of the valley. There were many secret hidey-holes under the lantana where Girija, Jayan and I had played with other children who lived in the estates.

The tuck shop was in the dining hall behind the children's hostels. This was at the other end of the valley from where we lived. Walking under the tall trees past the old guesthouse, I came to a sudden stop as a strange scene began to unfold. Before me was the graceful figure of an elderly man standing quiet, under the vast green canopy of the tall rain trees that lined the yard in front of the guesthouse. His white hair was long and he was dressed formally in loose white pants, a long khadhi kurta and a pale peach-coloured vest. He was standing absolutely still with his back to me, so I hesitated behind the mango tree, wondering if I would disturb him by walking past or if I should duck up the hills to my right and somehow get to the dining hall from the back. Then I saw a middle-aged woman heading towards us. Deep in thought as she walked, looking down at the bridge near the guesthouse, she was wearing a gorgeous green sari with a red border and red blouse, and her hair was secured in a knot at the nape of her neck. She looked confident and resolute as she walked along, but when she caught sight of the man, she faltered, then moved hastily towards him and fell to her knees to touch his feet.

I watched in surprise as the man hastily retreated a few paces and extended his arms in a gesture of supplication, pleading with the woman to stand up. There was such a show of regret on his face that I could not release my gaze. The two of them were so totally engaged that I was confident they would not notice me. So on impulse I made a dash for it, running past them while I wondered why the woman's gesture of respect had gone so awry. The elder's look of total dejection had come as a big surprise. It was not what I had come to expect. I wondered why he hadn't taken it as a compliment. All he seemed concerned about was for the woman to stand and not prostrate herself at his feet.

I gripped the shopping list in my fist and hurried over the bridge, running under a peepal tree, up the tarred road and past the medical dispensary to the dining hall. I could feel my heart pounding as I walked past the kitchens and around the back to where the tuckshop was almost hidden away in a large storage area of the building. The storeroom was lined from floor to ceiling with shelves filled with cardboard boxes, packages, tins and bottles. Standing on my tiptoes, I looked over the counter and called out to Captain Nair to hand him my father's list. The ex-captain had been a soldier in the Indian army, and when he had retired from the army he had come to work in Rishi Valley.

'Hello!' he called out in his deep gravelly voice before he spoke in Malayalam to ask if my mother had enjoyed her holiday with us. As he talked, he walked about the room from shelf to shelf, writing down the sought-after items in a book. Then he wrapped them up in some newspaper, tied the parcel carefully with some twine made from jute and handed me the package over the counter. Reaching up, I put my hand to my forehead in a salute, recalling the time he had shown us how to march and salute the flag as he'd done in the army. Captain Nair laughed affably as he made sure I had a good hold of the package. As I walked out into the sunlight, I heard him say, 'It is a long way back to your house, so stay in the shade as much as you can.'

'Yes, Captain,' I called as I ran down the road under the trees, holding the package close to my chest. I was still baffled by the scene I had witnessed by the bridge and I wondered if I would ever see the elderly man again. When I told my father of the strange incident, he laughed and said, 'Oh, that must be Krishnaji you saw. He is the only one I can think of who does not like people falling at his feet.'

I could not resolve myself to the look of despair I had witnessed on the elder's face, and my father's knowing laugh only deepened the mystery. The valley was an intriguing place, I thought. It was full of unusual people who never failed to surprise me.

Looking back at some games we children had choreographed earlier in the year, I reviewed my feelings and was embarrassed to admit that I had genuinely enjoyed the idea of people kneeling before me. In fact we had each coveted that role and competed over it. So why had the elderly gentleman reacted in despair?

Dancing Sticks

When I was seven, I went to audition to be a dancer. I was determined to be the best dancer in the world. To be the best, I knew that I had to start early in life.

'Every step, every gesture has a meaning,' said Meenakshi Akka, our dance teacher. She was sitting on the floor after showing us how to hold the backs of our hands on our hips and to stamp to the beat of her dancing sticks. The sticks, left on the floor beside her mat, were painted in bright red and green. I noticed that they were worn at the tips.

We had to take care that we did not bang our heels together as we stamped our feet. We also had to make sure that our knees were bent sideways. Standing still at half mast, holding my hands backwards against my hips, I began to regret my decision to come along to the class.

'Your back has to be as straight as a ruler,' she said, striking the sticks on the floor in front of her.

There were three other girls from junior school on the dance floor, all stamping sideways while she called out the rhythm of the dance step. My heels were hurting and my knees jarred with every stamp. I was so focussed on keeping my back straight, I forgot to breathe. There was a burning sensation in my chest, and my thighs were aching with the effort of maintaining such an ungainly stance. I looked at her, appealing, and stood up straight. She ignored me and kept beating her sticks while the other girls struggled to keep pace with the routine. As I stood aside, I could feel my heart beating loudly in my chest. The muscles in my back had never felt so taut, and I was feeling dizzy.

'Shoulders straight!' said the dance teacher sternly. 'Thaia, thy! Thaia, thy!' she instructed, in keeping with the beat of her sticks. Her posture was superb and she looked purposeful and completely absorbed in her task. She rapped her sticks alternately against each other and then onto the floor. I watched the green and red paint turn into a collage of colours as they met, separated and hit the floor. Meanwhile the girls stamped and stamped to the rhythm of her assertive instructions.

Did I really want to spend three mornings a week doing this, I wondered. It seemed such a long way to come to squat, my body halfway to the floor, and stamp sideways to the relentless beat of red and green sticks. Suddenly Meenakshi Akka ceased singing and smiled at the girls who were still dancing. She watched them, approving, as they too relaxed.

'You will be much better at the end of a couple of weeks of practice,' she said. And then she looked at me. I avoided her eyes, feeling awkward. I hadn't really kept up with the practice and didn't feel worthy of approval.

The practice was held early in the morning. I knew that by the time I got back home, showered and ate my breakfast, I would be late for assembly. So if I continued dance practice, I would be racing back and forth for an hour each day just to get to school on time. The floor on which we had all been stamping early that morning seemed to be a long way down now that I was looking at it with a cool head.

Meenakshi Akka rose gracefully from the mat. Picking up her sticks, she carefully set them to the side of the room. We helped to tidy up the place and picked our jumpers up from the floor. She was standing by the door as we queued to go past her.

I was last in line. I hung my head, unsure if I wanted to go on with the classes. Dancing was not as glamorous as it looked on stage. It had seemed a lot more fun inside my head than on the dance floor. From the way my body ached, dancing to the beat of sticks felt like torture.

'Geetha, you can always try music,' Meenakshi Akka said. I looked up at her in surprise. I had never thought about music or singing. There were two music rooms at the auditorium, full of traditional Indian string instruments. The place was treated with reverence not only because the instruments were expensive, but more because the music that came out of them was so immensely moving. As I walked past her, I nodded before I knew it. My shoulders straightened and I was out the door in a flash. She had implied in the kindest possible way that I would not be coming back.

Did I really want to let go of my plans to be the best dancer in the world, I wondered. I wrestled with the fact that my earlier resolve had been so weak. I ought to grit my teeth and pound my feet until I succeed, I thought. Otherwise I might succeed at nothing. Although I was grateful to her for giving me something to look forward to, I also felt as if I had let myself down. I remembered how excited I had been at the start of the lesson, and a feeling of shame and uncertainty swept over me.

As I walked away from the other girls who lived only a few yards from the dance room, I chose to retrace the path I had taken in the morning rather than take a shortcut through the bush. I remembered how purposeful I had been as I headed towards the class. I had been determined to do my best. Now there was only the strange and unexpected feeling of failure. The path was still clouded in shadow. Few people were about. It was also cold and misty at this time of year.

The dance and music were the best part of the school, my mother had told me when I wrote to her that I had decided to join the classes. She said she had never heard music so beautiful until she had attended a performance at our school. Visalakshi, the principal's wife, was a gifted musician. In fact, she was one of the best musicians anyone had heard. All the people in the valley were united in their opinion of her incredible talent. Perhaps I could learn from her when I got to senior school, I consoled myself. You had to be a senior to learn to play the veena and thambura. It would be amazing to play an ancient instrument as a gifted musician.

As I walked in through our front door my mind was teeming with new plans. My eyes were moving restlessly as if they did not know where to look. The same sense of excitement that I left with in the morning was now filling my head with new pictures of being a musician. I felt like a fraud at my own lack of conviction. How fickle were my feelings? One minute I was going to be a great dancer and the next I was going to be a brilliant musician. My mind filled with scenes of playing in front of an audience. New feelings for music flared in my heart. I remembered the melodious sound of children singing together in Sanskrit, with Mr Venks on Wednesdays. I imagined the beat of the drums, the sounds of the string instruments and the colourful silk saris the ladies wore as they led the whole school on a singsong in the auditorium on other days. The sights and sounds I recalled filled my mind with a feeling of intense beauty. It was really grand to sing harmoniously with hundreds of people in the mornings.

I wondered why I had never thought of learning to play music before. When the musicians played together, it was clear they were experts at their craft. Their music sounded so melodious as it floated through the valley. From the intensity of feeling that was on the musicians' faces, it was clear they poured their whole hearts into their work. Would I ever be able to play like that? It was amazing to just sit there and listen to them day after day, but it was strange to think of playing like them. When they played music together, they were tense and poised over their instruments, listening to the notes each made. They would look at each other and sometimes at us, making emphatic gestures of pure delight as they played. Did they know that they were playing with our feelings? Intense admiration swept over me as I realised how much I loved their music. Suddenly for some reason the scene had changed and my world had opened up to a new delight.

Now at home and undressing, I wrinkled my nose when I smelt the sweat on my tunic as it came off over my head. It was made of thick dark green cotton. As it fell in a heap on the floor, I shrugged off my dream of becoming the best dancer in the world. I ran to the shower so I could arrive on time for the morning assembly. We would be singing Sanskrit bhajans with Mr Venks before class. I had no desire to be late because the hall had no walls and everyone sitting inside would witness a late arrival. There was no place to hide from a hundred prying eyes. Besides, singing together was too good to miss, even if I did not always understand what we were singing about.

My ambition to become a great musician could wait until another day. I resolved that I would enjoy whatever music I could immerse myself in today, and listen carefully to our voices rising and falling in harmony.

Who is this I?

The air was cool in the morning and our whole school had been sitting for over an hour listening to a discourse between several people. I walked out of the hall feeling pins and needles in my feet from sitting cross-legged so long on the floor. I was surprised that I could stand up straight, and also stand aside to get out of the way of people heading towards the rows of slippers lining one wall of the music room. I could not remember where amid all those slippers I had left mine.

I stood by the pillars and watched as a well-dressed man walked up to me after donning his sandals.

'Did you enjoy the talk?' he asked with a broad smile.

I wondered what there was to enjoy as I felt my legs slowly coming back to life. Sitting on the floor for over an hour listening to him quizzing Krishnaji had certainly not been enjoyable. But I nodded my head all the same because I just wanted him to go away. He had gone on about the philosophy of the East and the West and had kept on quoting from different religious texts. We had no idea what he was talking about and it had washed over our heads. The dialogue had grown into a battle of wits, with Krishnaji trying to include the children while the scholar continued to use elevated speech beyond our comprehension.

Listening to the quotes rolling off his tongue, I had been astonished by the ease with which he'd produced complex phrases with well-rehearsed Urdu and Sanskrit rhyming words. I was really impressed. I was having enough trouble learning my nine-times table off by heart. (Seven had been easy to memorise because I was aged seven and mastering it had given me a feeling of real accomplishment.)

As I hesitated by his side, a senior student came up to us and they began talking. I watched as they walked down through the garden, heading towards the senior school. The older children knew how to make casual conversation with visitors to the school. They joked about politics, the financial news, Coca-Cola and new inventions that were transforming the world. I had heard a lot about the world on BBC radio broadcasts, so I was familiar with commentators talking about diplomatic relations and making important predictions about the future.

But Krishnamurti had asked this scholar to put all his clever quotes aside and just simply listen to the questions he had put to the school at the start of the talk that day. 'What is it to be educated? Was education about learning by exploring, or was it about accumulating knowledge?'

That morning, Krishnamurti had arrived after we had all been seated. Sitting down gracefully on the little podium with its thick cream cotton throw-over, he had remained silent for a while, allowing all of us to quieten and focus on listening. His body was slight and erect. He had large eyes which stood out in his beautiful austere face. He had a way of moving his eyes around the hall without overly moving his head. There had been a sense of immense intensity from the moment he posed the question that morning. It was buoyed by a touch of good humour which was evident as he gazed around at us. Watching his relaxed but erect posture made us want to straighten up and pay attention. We became aware of how we were watching, listening, sitting and breathing. Was my breathing quiet and steady, filling my lungs with oxygen and filling my brain with energy? Or was my breathing shallow and erratic?

'Posture is everything,' our yoga teacher would often say in the mornings. With good posture you could surpass anything, he believed. Making sure that the brain was filled with oxygen and that the lungs had plenty of space to expand and expel were all an essential part of living the 'right' way. Bad posture could bring about backaches, put pressure on our internal organs and bring about a whole array of digestive problems. Life wasn't something you could be lazy about. Looking at Krishnamurti, I admired his posture. They said that he had always done yoga. Even though he was older than my grandmother, he could still run lightly like a child. But despite my good intentions that morning to sit up and listen with all my heart, my attention had wavered because the conversation between the visiting scholar, a couple of members of staff and Krishnamurti had gone way over my head.

Suddenly, as if in despair, Krishnamurti had burst out with the words, 'Who is this I?' challenging the scholar to speak for himself for the first time that morning rather than quote endlessly from texts. The man had stopped short, taken aback.

'The self, sir!' he blustered, looking anxious, even while charged with an intention to put his point across. The rest of us sat back and watched an extraordinary sense of theatre unveiling in our midst. Marking the stress on the scholar's face, I looked back at Krishnamurti to see what had caused his reaction. Krishnamurti was laughing at the man's look of intense surprise.

'Have you ever seriously put that question to yourself, sir?' he asked with a poignant tone.

It suddenly occurred to me that the question could very well have applied to me, too. 'Who is this I?' I asked myself for the first time in my life. I was surprised that there should be such a question. The answer had seemed obvious until the question was raised. I was the presence that witnessed all that was going on. To imagine that there was something else besides made me feel intensely uncomfortable. I tried to look for something else to believe in, but the hall was emptying fast and the pillars and the concrete floor looked bare and could not hold my attention. I looked up at the white ceiling high above my head. Wherever I looked, the empty hall was filled with the question 'Who is this I?'

'Imagine if there really is no I!' I thought, trying to ward off a sense of uncertainty. 'What is real, if I am not real?'

Glancing about at the garden where I was walking, I checked to see all that was real. Everything around me seemed real enough. Now it was all so tangible, the walls of the school, the plants lining the road, the blue of the sky brightly visible through the dense canopy of flowering trees. Life was intensely real and fervently alive everywhere I looked.

Why had he implied that I did not exist ... or had he, I wondered. As my eyes rolled back in my head, I could not imagine how I could create a greater reality inside my head than what was around me. No amount of imagining could possibly create something more real than the world that existed all about me. I tried to make my surroundings go away, but no matter how hard I tried, I could not make the world disappear. The world I was walking in remained substantial and oozing with life.

'So who is this I?' I asked yet again. I watched inside as my eyes rolled to the back of my sockets to retrieve the sense of I. Yes, I could recall a name, a place of birth and the date I was born. They were all in the act of recall, and all I could really find. That was the universal I – a sense that everyone must be holding onto. Everyone had a name, a place of birth and a date of birth, I reasoned. But how did that really distinguish me from everyone else?

In all honesty, I confessed to myself wretchedly, I could only find that sense of self that everyone identified themselves by. A particular sense of myself, that which could be distinguished from all others, was nowhere to be found. Could I be lacking something significant? If so, what was I to do? What if everyone found out that I was lacking something substantial? Should I confide to my dad? What if he was disappointed? Moreover, what could he possibly do? Should I tell my friends that I lacked what was expected of me? What if they found me wanting?

My head would not stop clamouring for answers. I walked into the house and headed for the shower because I needed to wash away the tears streaming down my face before someone saw them. Perhaps I could cool off and figure out a way to cope with the problem that I'd suddenly found I faced. As the water washed down my back and through my long black hair, I resolved to keep this enigma all to myself. It was a secret, a dreadful secret, that I really had no 'I' other than an act of recall. What a dreadful plight I was in, I thought, clasping my hands together under the shower.

When I had run out of tears, from out of nowhere a string of words sprang to my mind with elegant simplicity. 'Live, love and learn.' Delighted, I felt a broad smile spread over my face. What a diplomatic solution! My heart rose and the lump in my throat began to dissolve. I marvelled at the words that had popped out of the blue.

The three Ls! That was what my education was about. I couldn't resist the grin that was spreading across my face. Surely that was it! The three Ls to balance the three Rs. I had to live, love and learn, to figure out what I was all about. I just had to watch to find out what I would be in a few years time. Such a pragmatic way to go about finding a solution. That way, no one would need to know that I had begun with nothing and I did not have to let anyone down. No wonder the BBC was always going on about diplomatic solutions. I was being silly tearing my heart over nothing. I was being impatient trying to find an 'I' to distinguish myself at the age of seven. I just had to bide my time, to live a little first … Surely that was the answer.

Reaching for the towel hanging over the door of the bathroom, I wrapped it round my wet hair and gave my head a vigorous rubdown. Then, as I ran down the corridor to the bedroom in search of my white cotton pyjamas, I heard the radio being turned on. As usual before dinner, dad was listening to the BBC evening news in the sitting room. Brushing my hair back from my eyes, I wondered why I had been so upset all day. It didn't seem to matter now that all I could find to distinguish myself from the rest of life was the memory of a name, a place and a date of birth.

My anxiety earlier in the day wasn't something I would forget in a hurry, I said to myself, feeling slightly smug.

So what was my problem? Why had I anguished about it all day?

I was surprised that I was able to let go of the anguish through a simple pragmatic insight which had come out of nowhere. My mind had come up with an understanding that I only had to recall in order to identify the 'I'.

Freedom in the Hills

It was Saturday afternoon and since I was free to do as I pleased on weekends, I had sought out my former playmate, Lakshmi, in the hope that we could play a game of hopscotch in the hills while everyone else was having a siesta. We were playing in the shade of a haystack piled up on a sloping granite slab, the yellow-grey stack over two metres high, to provide sufficient fodder for cattle all the year round. We were mimicking each other's movements, dancing as the sun burned down on us.

I asked her how she wanted to dance, imagining a tribal dance or the more traditional Bharathnatyam, but also thinking rather wistfully of dancing like a modern rock star. She looked at me in surprise, as if my question was quite incomprehensible to her. I felt a little taken aback by her reaction to my polite enquiry. Lakshmi would be about nine by now, I thought, being a year older than me. I wondered if she was being bossy because she was older, or simply offended by my suggesting a choice since it made her feel inferior.

'What kind of dance, what movement?' she answered back, thrusting her hips out a little and adopting a pose of interrogation. 'Which way do we dance?'

I was impressed by her stance. Lakshmi looked so assured and magnificent in her righteous indignation. Her red and gold glass bangles tinkled around her wrists as she gestured in my direction, including me imperiously in her scheme of things. As I heard the bells on her anklets, I looked at the orange design pigmented on her feet as well as her many silver toe-rings.

'You want to know everything, is that right? That's your problem. In the village the elders say that when you all start going to school you get too much stuff in your heads and then you walk with your heads in the air. Just watch me and do as I do. It's quite simple really.'

She tossed her hair from her face, twirled on her toes, tripped and fell down near me. We laughed, lying beside each other looking up at the sky. I remembered how we used to fool around before I began school, and wondered what had happened to me. How had I lost that wonderful sense of vitality?

'Do you have any classes today or are you free to play?' she asked in a confiding tone, turning her head to look at me. There was a pause. She was conceding that she would like company.

Interested, I smiled, moving my eyebrows up and down and making a cheeky face. Thankfully she had dismissed my dumb question about how best to move while dancing. She had put it behind us and now we could move on. I was really grateful for that.

We had changed such a lot in just a few months. I had been at school for a couple of years when we first met whereas Lakshmi had never been to school. Her parents lived in the village in the hills to the south and it was unlikely that she would ever go to school, as there weren't any schools there. My father had explained to me that the area was sparsely populated and it was unlikely that the state government would be willing to provide school facilities in the near future.

Lakshmi would look after her family's goats, and work in the fields growing groundnuts and millet like the daughters of my daycare mother. Then one day she would marry and move away. It all sounded like a fairy tale. Luckily for the moment, we were too young to be married. We still had a few years to go before puberty. Once girls became women, my daycare mother Papul Amma had said, most of the village parents preferred to get their daughters married quickly. That was the custom. It was considered the right thing to do.

Leaning back on to her hands as she sat on the granite slope, Lakshmi said, 'I have all day. All I have to do is watch the goats. You don't have to know what they do. You just watch and they take care of themselves mostly.'

Earlier, I had been a little nervous about the goats going astray and she'd tried to hide her surprise at my startling ignorance about herding goats. I looked a little abashed and then smiled so as not to disrupt our sense of camaraderie. We paused yet again, sizing each other up and testing the ground hesitantly. The goats pranced away as she threw a small branch in their direction. There was another mound of hay stacked under a tin roof where the workers sheltered from the midday sun when they were working in the hills. There was a lot of grass that had flown about in the wind. The prickly bushes growing in the vicinity were covered in these stray strands and the goats spent their time nibbling deliberately on these.

'I'm not breaking any rules,' Lakshmi reassured me, sensing that I was aware that the hay belonged to the school. 'The loose grass belongs to the hills and we have feeding rights here too, you know, just like the school. These are our traditional grounds.'

I nodded and stepped inside the circle she had marked in dots on the flat rock face using some stray pebbles. She smiled as I acquiesced.

'Watch where you go and I'll follow as you duck in and out of the circle. Then we can change roles and then we'll go on from there!'

We danced as we moved through the design marked by the pebbles, striking strange poses. When she swayed her hips, I pranced like a man stamping the ground in the affirmative. We laughed and continued to invent demons, angels, monkeys, frogs and peacocks to add to the repertoire of our movements. Miming each other and striking poses for entertainment, we challenged each other to hold these eccentric postures. Taking turns to lead and follow, I was amazed at the range of moves we could create together in this way.

I watched her bright crimson skirt swirling around her ankles. She had yellow ribbons braided into her hair and her crimson blouse was lined with a gold border to match the border on her skirt.

'Some of the goats have bells too, and we can use one of those tin cans to make music later on,' she called, leading me up the hill away from the hay stack.

'With different rocks, we can create a loud clatter in the tins,' she laughed. I had heard the sound before and had often wondered where it came from. Now I knew, and laughed with her. She would clatter during 'rest time' when the valley went quiet, and she could rouse a real racket. I wondered if she envied the wealthy kids who attended the boarding school. Was this possibly a way of getting back at them? Thinking of the grumbles I had heard from those who could afford a 'rest time', I looked at her with renewed admiration. Lakshmi was capable and carefree, and seemed quite unconcerned by the state of the world.

What a free spirit, I marvelled, and wished I had such an untroubled mind. Mine, I realised, had become shy, hesitant and doubtful, finding its way furtively through a myriad of rules and regulations.

How do I do this? How do I do that? Am I right? Am I wrong? Such questions lurked in my mind all the time. They would set off a flicker of anxiety in my chest, and I was always worrying about causing offence or nervous about being in the wrong, whereas I could see that she hadn't changed much at all. I watched her careless abandonment in body and mind, recalling how we used to play when we first got together.

Was her confidence the result of not attending school, I wondered enviously. School was supposed to be good for me. People spent enormous amounts of money to educate their children, to set them up for a successful life. Her parents had no money and yet she was happy and carried herself with poise and assurance.

What was happening to me? Was there something sinister going on? Was this why Krishnamurti urged us to watch ourselves and find out what happened to us through conditioning? My father had never been to school either. He was self-taught and had been apprenticed as a nurse in a boarding school in Sri Lanka before coming to work at the school. He too had an independent streak which I admired. I could sense that this quality was slowly but surely subsiding in me.

Lakshmi showed me some terracotta and ceramic chips that she used to play hopscotch with her friends. As the day wore on, she showed me how to balance things on my head and we walked around on uneven ground, poised to keep the chips from falling off our heads. Every now and then we dropped everything and raced among the boulders for fun, delighting in startling the goats as they wandered among us oblivious of the pebbles we had laid out to mark out our playground. Although we were engrossed in our games, I noticed that she was vigilant and careful not to lose sight of her herd.

'There's plenty to do up here even though I can't read or write,' she said, trying to bridge the gulf between us. She was examining a chip of granite which sparkled in the sunlight. Granite boulders loomed over our heads, making our postures seem exaggerated and theatrical, lending a quality of sublime timelessness that we could not conjure up by ourselves.

It was customary for children to have a few favourite rocks. Many of us gathered them and hid them in little stashes around the valley. She cast aside the one she had been examining.

'Once, up high, I found a little stash of these, hidden under the root of an old windswept stump of a tree,' she said. 'They might have been put there hundreds of years ago by another goatherd like me!'

Humbled by the notion of vast time, we looked up the hill and wondered at the passage of years from ancient times to the present. The hills were dry and bare and sparsely covered by green bushes. Had dinosaurs wandered over this landscape, I wondered, fascinated by the thought.

The goats did not seem to mind the thorns but we had to dodge between bushes, always mindful of being scratched. My feet were bare and silent but her anklets still made a tinkling sound as we ran towards the top of the hill. She moved lithely with a confidence that I could not match. She wasn't competitive and was always mindful of where I was. The dexterity of my body intrigued me as it climbed and crawled and clambered among the boulders on the top of the hill where the landmass gave way to the bright blue sky. My body did not need to know 'how' to do things, I realised. It just did them. Yet I still watched myself, surprised as I jumped, twirled, and raced with the goats on an uneven surface that I had not been on before.

Looking at the valley unfold below, I was surprised by the different perspective we had from above. There was plenty of time for reflection. As the goats grazed we lay watching the clouds float grandly by from one end of the valley to the other. We wondered what it would be like to ride on those spectacular clouds. Through the stream of fluffy white clouds, I caught sight of the sickle moon adamantly retaining its shape in the sky.

Later that day after we'd parted, I noticed that I fell into a false rhythm of walking like a model. One weekend I had seen the high-stepping artificial walk of vogue models in a documentary show on fashion. Watching the way my body fell into the graceful walk I had seen on screen, I was struck by how tense my muscles felt in conforming to a posture which was admired by so many people who watched the media. My back was straight, my head held high, and my toes were lining up to meet the ground each time. I tried to relax, to shrug off my habit, but it was hard to get rid of that fashionable pose. It felt as if my mind and body were at odds with each other.

I felt awkward as I walked along barefoot, trying to conform to an image of a high-heeled walk. I was struck by the implications of her freedom and my obvious desire to control my walk. Up there in the hills as we'd moved heedlessly, our bodies had been lithe and lively. It was shocking to realise how surreptitiously habits of thought had crept into my mind and simply taken over the movement of my whole body.

'Observe!' I could hear Krishnamurti's voice in my head. 'Observe the impact of labels on your mind.'

Perhaps my awkwardness was the result of conforming too much to social pressures instead of noticing their impact on me.

The Banyan Tree

The dance floor under the large banyan tree was made of grey polished concrete. The stage was wrapped around the main trunk and the massive tree stood as a grand backdrop. It was an open-air theatre set in the wilderness. Where were the monkeys that usually hung off the banyan's branches? Perhaps they had retreated to the hills for the day.

It felt good to be alone, to be able to hear the birds in the trees. I could also hear the estate workers calling in the distance. Standing on the ground in front of the raised stage, I felt rather small and humble; the great banyan had inspired the feeling in me. The tree was hundreds of years old, while I was merely eight. I wondered what it must feel like to be so old. Age and wisdom were linked in my mind.

What would it feel like to dance on that stage in front of the elders of our community? I'd seen children dancing on the polished floor in the evenings before. They would dance to live music as they practised for the end of year performance when Krishnamurti would return to our school. He would sit in the audience for a change instead of being the guest of honour on the platform, and watch the dancing with the rest of us.

The school was proud of its rich cultural heritage which spanned thousands of years to the Vedic traditions. Here there was a strong emphasis on Karnatik music, sport, dance and yoga, and a great respect for learning. This respect was a common heritage which enabled people from different parts of India to work together in mutual understanding. We shared the same stories and had a common understanding of the value of traditional cultures. Many of us spoke a range of languages but at school we relied on English. The songs we sang in the morning were in Sanskrit and Kannada, and I felt elated singing with others. We sang simply for the joy of singing; I couldn't understand the meaning of the words, but that didn't seem to matter. What really mattered was the feeling of singing together while musicians played the veena, tambura and tabla.

As I looked up at the canopy of the great banyan and down to its long dangling roots, I walked as far as the granite slabs that had been erected beneath the roots at some distance from the main trunk. One of the estate workers had mentioned that these slabs would be packed with rich soil in hessian bags to guide the roots all the way to the ground. This way they would make sure that the roots would grow into strong columns to support the wide span of the branches above.

I thought about how that the tree had grown in a forest once. It stood now at the centre of a school that was working to bring about a revolution in education. When the school's founders were looking for its site, they had seen the tree from as far away as the hills. They knew it provided proof there was sufficient ground water in the valley to support their education scheme. No one could have imagined that the school would thrive and grow so well; it had seemed such a wistful dream at first.

Now that the school had become established, people visited from far and wide to see what had been accomplished, and most were impressed by the idyllic scene they encountered. Places of learning were honoured by the Vedic tradition, but there was a key difference about our school that few realised. The difference was to do with authority.

When Krishnamurti suspended authority while speaking with the children, many onlookers indulged it as a passing phase, a gimmick of some sort. He was a great man and he was allowed to be somewhat eccentric. They did not realise that each time he pointed to the absence of authority, something in us became alert because he was challenging us to check things out for ourselves. If he had no authority and we were interpreting his words, then the onus for interpreting fell on us.

So I began to test what was said with care. I listened somewhat sceptically and then went away and began to reflect on the things I had heard and understood. If he had no authority, then it was up to me to make sure that what he said made sense. It was no longer a matter of merely following his words. I had to engage with the message and make sure it was true. That was the vital difference. By denying authority, Krishnamurti was enabling us to experience the wonder of our own innate capacity to gather information. He spoke about the concerns he had about the world. He enquired into the problems, the contradictions. He focused our attention on the unpleasant things about life that we had grown to ignore.

Children rarely get an opportunity to challenge authority. I had felt emboldened within minutes of hearing him deny his authority. It had been an extraordinary couple of years for me. Now, for the first time in my life, I had begun to reflect on my thoughts. I watched the way I interpreted what was being said. I became familiar with the feeling of listening and making sense.

Before arriving at the school, I used to take what was said 'on board', and my mind would simply run with it. I used to ignore large chunks of what I heard and deal only with what concerned me most. Compared to that, listening, reflecting and checking things out for myself required a lot of serious effort on my part. It made me feel that I was alive and fully engaged in learning about life. This reawakened my interest in learning.

By denying authority, Krishnamurti had effectively restored my sense of autonomy. I wasn't being told what to do and I could no longer blindly follow what was said. I was made responsible for checking for myself. If I did not understand, it was up to me to clarify my mind. I could talk to my father, or my Ayah, or perhaps a friend. I was amazed by the difference this made to my world. Suddenly that world opened up.

Now I knew I could not rely on authority to tell me what to think, feel or see, and there was no room for complacency. I had to discover things afresh. Although I could not rely on authority, I didn't suspect for a moment that I could not rely on intelligence.

Life was tangibly, palpably filled with intelligence. It filled my world and brought me to my senses. I had nothing to be wary of, I realised. I simply had to be aware. For the first time in my life, I realised that awareness is all-embracing.

Free Rangers

A few of my friends and I were walking through the valley during the holidays, feeling as if we were missing out on the good things in life. Most of our friends had gone to stay with their families in the big cities around India to escape the heat of the Deccan Plateau and get a flavour of modern life, but most of our parents were members of staff who had made the valley their home.

Yes, we were feeling sorry for ourselves because at the ages of nine to twelve, we wanted to experience a 'real holiday'. One classmate had said she was going to a city fun park where there were giant slippery dips for hair-raising rides and glitz galore. Not to be outdone, we were scouting around for something equally exciting to do.

The valley seemed sleepy without the hustle and bustle of children. There were no teachers calling out, minding time and fussing about keeping to a regular schedule. We looked up at the large copper bell which was hung on a large tamarind tree between the junior and senior school buildings. It was covered in rust and was unusually silent. The thought did cross our minds, but we didn't think it would help our cause to pull the long rope and send the notes echoing back from the hills.

We decided that we needed a nickname, an identity. A heated conversation about what to call ourselves followed: Freedom Fighters, Tarzan, Lone Ranger, maybe The Three Musketeers. Not likely ... there were six of us so the numbers just didn't add up. How inconvenient! We were the Free Rangers, we decided. It had a touch of hype and added a bit of jazz. It was not gender-specific and had something to do with freedom. That had to be good, surely?

To assert our freedom, we decided to go out of bounds. Beyond the signpost to the school, there was a hill with a slope called 'sliding rock'. From a distance it looked as if it had a smooth slant where we could take a practice run and see if it lived up to its name. It felt like the sort of thing 'Free Rangers' would do. We planned to gather some cuttings from the shrubs by the road. We could use these as padding in case the ride wasn't particularly smooth, because it wouldn't help to return with torn clothes after playing truant. On the way up, we discussed the kids who went to the cities for their holidays with some envy, and I got the feeling that our isolation gave us a sense of solidarity. There was no use hanging about. We were going to set things right. No one else was going to help us have an exciting time, so we decided we'd better find our own thrills.

We picked out some lush vegetation and stacked it into bundles, making sure that there were no itchy plants to cause remorse later on. We tied the branches together with twine from coconut palms, and the bundles all held together wonderfully and looked ever so green. There were a few scuffles and mock altercations to liven up our day. Then we set out with bravado, each shouldering a strategic buffer for the everlasting slide of our lives.

Emerging into the open on the outskirts of the valley, we looked up at the sliding rock. I felt a little uneasy, but dismissed my thoughts sternly. We were too far gone to change our minds. We had to stick to our plan. It had sounded so cool and it was still a good plan, I thought. We trudged up the slope along a narrow rocky path and followed each other to the top where the massive rock had been cut and flattened into slabs to be used as building blocks for our school. Like many hills in the area, most of the rocks that were easily accessible were quarried for granite building blocks.

Although the rock had looked smooth from a distance, on closer inspection we realised that the surface was covered in rubble left behind by the stonemasons. We hugged our lush padding close to our chests and finally made it to the top.

'This is going to be fun, but it is hard work getting up here,' I panted, fossicking for reasons not to repeat the exercise. Looking at my mates, it was comforting to realise that I wasn't the only one who was having second thoughts.

But it was important not to hold back, if only to keep our identity. If we were careful, we could have our fun and save our knickers as well. The sun was going down in a blaze of colour behind the dark blue hills of Rishi Konda. There was no plausible reason for us to hold off our descent any longer. We checked each other out.

'Yippee, yahoo,' we shouted, thinking of John Wayne and Clint Eastwood to stir up a sense of excitement. The incline did not look safe from the top, as the surface was far from smooth. We sat down gingerly on our lush padding, which was beginning to wilt, and tried to skid down the hill. Some of us did manage to propel forward for a couple of feet. Others got stuck on a wedge in a rock and strategically stayed put. Our leader who had gone further up than us started an unexpected avalanche of loose rubble. We looked up in dismay as fresh-cut shards of granite tumbled randomly down the slope. Blue sparks flew from the edges of the rocks as they rolled past us. A couple of boys changed plans and decided to throw stones against the slant to see if they could get them to spark.

Listening to the stones bouncing past us towards the bottom of the hill, we decided it was a good time to leave. I could feel the graze on my arm burning. As I looked down at the landscape stretching in every direction, the pain in my arm was suddenly eclipsed by the beauty rolling out before my eyes. The landscape seemed sublime and so magnificently unconcerned by our plight. It was a vast and immovable stretch into the blue distance, embraced by a sky that was turning golden in the setting sun. Our lack of accomplishment felt inconsequential in the face of such a panorama of lights and shadows playing on the contours of the land.

That was a close shave, we thought, holding our devil-may-care expressions intact. Our minds were on other things, though. Nature was a formidable force, but, oh, we weren't fazed by its unpredictable ways. We looked at each other, noticing the mixed emotions written on our faces. Implicit in our stance was the fact that it had been our plan, so we were going to stick by each other no matter what. Meanwhile the light on the hills played with our feelings.

We looked up at the rough-hewn rock and thanked our lucky stars. We threw away the mashed up vegetation, hoping some goats would feast on it and get rid of the evidence. It was time to get a move on. It had been a good idea, but we had not accounted for gravity. Gravity had won over our fanciful ideas. Life had a mean and unrelenting streak; it had lured us up there and let us down.

If one of us had been knocked out, it would have been disastrous, I realised as we were reaching the bottom of the hill. There could have been all kinds of consequences. It would have taken hours to get to a hospital and we would have been in a lot of strife. Picking our way gingerly down the last slope, we then made our way across a gully in single file to get back to the road. We walked along the tarred road past a field of sunflowers to the school gardens where we could welcome the feeling of enclosure as the gathering gloom of twilight slowly covered the valley.

'Why do they call it Sliding Rock?' asked one boy as he headed towards the pond. Maybe we should call it Slippery Slopes, somebody suggested. Some loser must have called it Sliding Rock, and we'd been conned, someone else decided. What a sick sense of humour! Had they done that on purpose?

As we cleaned up by the pond, we counted our bruises and maintained what we imagined were 'stiff upper lips'. The skin on our knees was in tatters but our reputation was intact. We were still the Free Rangers. But we winced as we examined our cuts and grazes.

We would lie low for a while to heal our bodies and egos. Perhaps we could make some pretty garlands, or practice drawing patterns in the yards with white rice powder. But we would not let ourselves be misguided by words again. It was risky to rely on someone else's description.

Perhaps that was what Krishnamurti meant when he emphasised, 'The description is not the described.' We had fallen for a name, and our day had certainly not gone according to plan – but we still had each other.

Role Play

My cousin Jayan and I were playing with my sister Girija in the living room. She was six – three years younger than us – and just starting school. It was holiday time and my mother had brought my sister and our cousin to visit for several weeks.

We decided she could play the role of Queen Victoria and sit in a chair with a rod in her hand looking very haughty, in an elaborate game we devised to while away the afternoon.

Jayan wanted to be a villain who was caught and brought to justice because in the Malayalam movies that he watched, villains had so much power. I decided to be the minister who would advise the Queen. We found some ropes to tie up the villain and discussed what he had done wrong, but we couldn't decide on the appropriate punishment. After quarrelling over the worst crimes and the best punishments, we were no longer in a mood to play the game.

Just then my father, Cha, breezed in through the front door, calling out to my mother who was in their bedroom reading a Malayalam magazine. Amma liked spending her holidays on the school estate where we lived because she could get away from her daily routine of cooking, teaching and cleaning her house in the evenings. Here she could mix with a group of educated people from different parts of the world who had come to assist Krishnamurti in setting up the school which he said would create a revolution in education.

My father was surprised to see us sitting with our backs to each other.

'What's the problem? Why such long faces?' he asked. My mother was frowning as she walked into the living room. She glanced at my father.

'Here!' she said, handing me a magazine with a lot of writing and a few cartoon pictures. 'Make up some random punishments and put them in a basket to use in your games. Punishments are based on rules, not handed out on a whim. You have to follow rules and proper procedures. Otherwise you will be fighting forever and that will spoil the game.'

'Queen Victoria had rules and she stuck by them,' my father added. 'That's why the British were so successful in conquering the world.'

Jayan responded enthusiastically and offered to make scrolls of manuscripts. Amma helped him cut the pages into long narrow strips, asking us to make a list of plausible punishments. Earlier in the day she had helped to make a wreath of orange marigolds for Girija to wear as a crown. This was secured on her head at an odd angle with hairpins that she kept rearranging. I had on a long garland of jasmine and the distinctive smell of flowers was wafting up my nostrils. Jayan had a rakish red scarf round his neck to look like a villain.

We were making a list of punishments such as, 'Off with his head,' 'Ten years in jail,' 'Thirty days without food,' as my father regaled us with the events of the day at the dairy farm, including the news that a visitor to the school had dropped by the farm. The man was from America, my father told us, using an important tone. Democracy flourished in the United States, he explained, because the government was genuinely interested in looking after the needs of the people. The man who came to see him had a PhD and worked in the Department of Agriculture. The USDA was founded in President Lincoln's time, my father remarked, looking impressed. That was over a hundred years ago! No wonder it was such a great nation, he added with conviction, nodding emphatically as he looked at all of us.

The visitor had praised the health of our cows, the fields of guinea grass and lucerne and, curiously, the number of people assisting my father in the dairy. The visitor had also explained that the economies of scale had tipped the balance in favour of mechanisation in the United States so that farmers could no longer afford to hire people to milk their cows. My father made a wry face of theatrical bewilderment.

Amma was never too interested in hearing about the West, let alone worrying about how cows were treated, so while they bickered over the rights of cows to be milked by hand, I returned to the onerous task of writing out appropriate punishments.

Blindfolding and throwing Jayan into a dungeon for a month sounded rather nice, I whispered to my sister, and she nodded, smiling conspiratorially. So we grabbed the white cotton ropes that Cha used in the dairy to harness his cows and set to work on our cousin. Jayan allowed us to tie his hands behind his back and we also made sure his feet were tied securely so he would have to beg us for mercy. Wriggling on the floor, Jayan made up a long story about a crime he had committed in Mayyanad where the ration shopkeeper stored all his wares. Queen Victoria ordered me to find the right punishment and I foraged through the scrolls to find the one labelled 'the dungeon'.

Running through a few scenarios, we were impressed by how inventive Jayan had been in his villainous acts. We began to sense a sneaking respect for his ingenuity and almost wanted to applaud him for his crimes instead of punishing him. But the list would come to our assistance and we fell into a routine, taking turns to play by the rules we had set. As the afternoon wore on, my parents retired for their siesta, and I realised that my head was spinning with all the ideas that were flitting through my brain.

Since Krishnamurti had urged us to observe the movement of thought, I had begun to notice how my mind jumped from topic to topic, crafting ideas to cater to my increasing appetite for making sense of everything. By the end of a couple of hours playing different roles, my head was blazing with conflicting scenarios. There were so many contradictions in all our plots. Increasingly the basket was coming to our rescue as the manuscripts helped, by default, to sort out the main area of contention, which was how to best punish each other for the crimes we had committed.

As my mother had implied, the best way to keep the game going was to consult the manuscripts in the basket ... to follow the rules and methods used previously.

It occurred to me that perhaps this is what Krishnamurti had meant when he spoke of a need for a revolution in thinking to reduce inner conflict.

Eavesdrop and Hoodwink

My sister Girija and I were making our way back home for lunch. On a rather hot afternoon, walking past the post office then down the steep incline towards the old guest house, we paused to catch our breath near the little granite bridge. The laundry yard was filled with row upon row of white cotton bed sheets flapping in the breeze. They were stretched over the yard in neat rows as if basking in the light reflected from the white clouds above.

Girija seemed a little tired. Three years younger than me and still in junior school, her seventh birthday was coming up. The sun was very hot along that particular stretch of the road, without any trees for shade, so I decided the best thing to do was to weave a story to get her mind off the long walk home.

'Eavesdrop and Hoodwink went for a walk,' I announced, leading her on. She smiled, to indulge my jaunt into fantasy. The cue was right. I could run riot with our imaginations and we would find ourselves at home in no time at all. Relieved, I clutched at imaginative straws to string along an interesting story line. I had heard about 'Shangri-La' and the word

'Utopia' had cropped up among my friends. I wondered what it must be like to live in such a place. Would cities be built in the sky some day, up in the clouds? If I could hoodwink her into imagining a scintillating dome, I might just get us home.

My mind filled with possibilities. I described in great detail my castle in the air. The walls were made from crystal that would change colour like a chameleon. At the flick of a switch it would change its hues to match the sunset or disguise itself amidst the blue hills which seemed to bear down on us in the distance.

She gave me a non-committal look. It wasn't going to be easy I realised; she wasn't going to be pliable. Her eyes looked too keen and her stride was too firm, yet the castle loomed large in my mind, winking with possibilities. I invited her to describe a room in the mythical castle. That would surely keep her mind occupied, I thought. It might also buy me some valuable time to invent something more to captivate her mind.

In the heart of this castle, we decided, was a giant loom. Our father's family were weavers in Mayyanad and we had often watched our aunts and uncles at their old wooden loom as they flicked the shuttle back and forth through the vast array of threads stretched across planks. Many colourful brocades were woven here for weddings, funerals, births and festivals. The patterns were steeped in mystery, I assured her. Many, many centuries of skills had gone into weaving the cloth and designing the patterns. Someone in our father's family would have had the secret codes for each design.

Checking her out for some response, I realised that I wasn't going to strike it lucky. She looked rather bored, her brow was elevated and her eyes drooped in a weary expression that she was barely trying to conceal. My heart fell. I was falling in love with my utopia but for some unknown reason, she would not come on board. Luckily we were nearly home. The sun was still hot and we were getting very thirsty.

'The water in the palace can be piped in straight from the clouds and so it is crystal clear,' I ad-libbed to keep her engaged for the last few hundred metres. 'They have a machine that captures dew!' Hardly likely, I thought secretly to myself, hoping she wouldn't give this idea much thought.

'What about the sewers?' she sprang at me, much to my surprise.

I tried to hide my annoyance. What on earth did sewers have to do with Utopia? What an untimely remark that was. How inconvenient and how grossly insensitive of her. She ought to know better. I glared at her dismissively. Why couldn't she just wander along and enjoy my fantasy? I dropped back in a huff and watched her walk away disdainfully. She had a spring in her step as if she was enjoying her solitude.

Behind me I heard the familiar voice of Mr Mark Lee, my junior school teacher, walking past the tamarind trees by the post office. He was chatting with a founder of our school, Mr Achyut Patawardhan, as they came out of an important staff meeting with Krishnamurti.

'This year he's been talking a lot about preparing the ground to liberate intelligence from the authority of the known,' I heard Mark Lee say in his distinctive American accent.

Achyut Patawardhan nodded in agreement. They were walking side-by-side, pondering the morning's events.

'I have no idea how,' said Mr Patawardhan. 'Hopefully he will explain, and if he succeeds, perhaps the children will tell us one day. Who knows, then the world might be free. There may never be another world war like the ones we've seen this century.'

They were looking at each other, wincing at the thought of the wars they had lived through. I could feel their despair. I watched them carefully, wondering why they were somewhat baffled. Coming to a parting of their ways, they bade each other a friendly goodbye and walked away, both deep in thought.

I stopped, dumbstruck. They had really meant what they'd said and were not just making polite conversation. Could we really stop world wars from happening? Could we really transform the world simply by observing our minds as we were growing up?

What a strange thought. Surely they had to be joking. But no, they were indeed serious. They had spoken earnestly and had sounded very concerned about the state of the world. They had obviously been at a staff meeting where Krishnamurti had explored a different approach to education. My father and our neighbours, the Moorheads, had often implied that Krishnamurti was convinced that education could make an enormous difference by enabling children to explore their psychological make-ups, as they engaged in learning about the world from both within and without. In ignoring the processes involved in learning, a conditioned mind came to rely deeply on prior knowledge, following tradition blindly without questioning. This ignorance of the nature of the human mind and the readiness to rely on leaders such as Hitler and Mussolini had been responsible for war, the two men believed. They spoke with a conviction that something could be done, and should be done, to ensure such crimes against humanity would never occur again. To me it was clear that they were tantalised by the prospect of a different kind of education which allowed children the freedom to explore the movement of thought.

But what did Krishnaji mean by the phrase 'liberating intelligence from the authority of the known,' I wondered.

Liberation sounded so good that the very thought sent a sense of longing tugging at my heart. But the thing that puzzled me was that Krishnamurti's approach implied that we all had intelligence. He spoke as if he was drawing on our intelligence. That was a fresh start, for sure. I had no problem with that. It was a refreshing change from the norm. The other teachers were tacitly setting us up against each other because in the conventional classroom we were inevitably competing with each other with 'correct' knowledge. The teachers had to grade us at the end of term – we were inadvertently ranked in their eyes – but Krishnaji's regard was forthright, eager and wholly committed to an inquiry into learning.

As for 'authority of the known', I had no idea what he meant. I wanted the world to be perfect, just as I had wanted my utopia to be perfect. It had seemed so easy to invent a utopia, but even in that I had failed miserably. Baffled by the complexity of the world, I decided all I could do was take life a step at a time. I wandered past the laundry and on towards the bullock yard, still keeping my sister in sight.

Girija had a point about Utopia, I admitted reluctantly. What did they do about the sewers? Did Utopia have to have one or was waste miraculously taken care of somehow? Perhaps the angels were really plumbers in disguise. What a vexing problem sewers were, I thought, feeling deflated. It was an inconvenient fact that I had preferred to overlook. I wished sewers would take care of themselves instead of upsetting my dreams.

My notion of a perfect world had been so convenient to conjure up but my little sister had an inconvenient eye for detail. She had been quick to realise that my story was too far removed from reality. She had seen right through the flaws in my storyline. I couldn't help but admire her insight.

Trying to retrieve my bruised ego, I shuffled on home. It was sad that the world was not perfect, as I had envisaged it. Just because the name 'utopia' existed, this did not mean the place existed, I counselled myself. My mind stopped fretting after a while. My sister had given me a reality check, and it was funny when I thought about it in hindsight.

On second thoughts, I was rather glad she hadn't let me get away with my fantastic story of living in the clouds with the giant looms. I rather enjoyed the fact that I had my feet planted firmly on the ground. As I got close to our house, I could hear the BBC world news from across the lawn. There were growing concerns about the price of oil due to world supplies dwindling, and the impact of pollution around the world. The IRA was not giving up easily and there were more bombs being exploded randomly. Politicians talked a great deal about change but no one had an answer for the violence.

After putting my books on the shelf in the living room, I went to the kitchen to get a drink of water. Everything sounded so officious on the radio. How did the BBC get it right all the time? On whose authority did they hold forth with such assurance? My story had fallen apart so easily. How did their journalists manage to spin their tales so effectively? It was all about the real world, they always implied ... or was it? To me, the world sounded such a complex place to live in, smouldering with an intent to kill and bristling with menacing threats and allegations. I wondered if there was a catch in a news story just as there had been in mine. Had the journalists missed something we might discover so we wouldn't have to go on living with war? Would the different power blocks ever clean up their act so we could all finally live in peace? Listening to the news, it did not seem very likely. Even the hope that things would improve one day sounded vain and ridiculous to me.

I had lost faith in my imaginative castles in the air, but I hadn't yet found any alternative that was satisfactory. I hadn't yet discovered what Krishnamurti really meant about freeing the mind from 'the authority of the known'.

A Suitable School

'If thoughts are left unchecked to run riot in this manner, what is to say that pure mayhem will not follow? Children need an education. They need to be taught to think properly, not to think what they like or to be free from thought.'

Unusually for South India, the woman who was holding forth strode in front of her husband. Her silk sari with gold brocade along its border swished as she passed, the intricate patterns unfolding to the sunlight with every move she made. Aged about fifteen, I was fascinated by the sparkles of her toe rings and bangles, and wondered how many sovereigns of gold she wore on her arms. My sister was a little hesitant about the woman's belligerent manner, and we hung back a little so we would not be noticed yet could stay within earshot.

We had seen the couple walking around the valley for a few days. They seemed to be from abroad. No doubt looking for a 'suitable' school for their son, my dad had said, raising his eyebrows as we described in detail all the finery the lady was wearing. Like us, he often fielded questions about the school when visitors came to stay at the new guest house down the road from our home.

As the husband walked past us, I could see that he was deep in thought. He looked anxious and unconvinced. It was as if he was aware that the final decision rested with his wife.

'He will be safe in this environment, he will have a good education and we need not worry about him for years,' he said, appealing to his wife, hurrying after her, entreating her to listen to him, to be reasonable and just hear him out for a change. But his plea fell on deaf ears. His wife was poker-faced and determined to have her way. Her back was stiff and she did not hesitate as she headed up the curved driveway towards the guest house.

As I listened, I wondered why it was so important for him to educate his son at the school. This whole question of education seemed to stir such strong emotions in people. Sometimes the behaviour of parents showed that they were incredulous about the values the school stood for. Often they would fume and gesticulate, or clear their throats mightily, as they strove to elaborate their views. They wanted to have the final say, to justify their points of view and to clear their consciences all at once, and yet they were beguiled by the notion of 'transformation in education' that was associated with the school's philosophy. They were transported by the idea of serenity and psychological wellbeing. Over the years, my sister and I had heard some heated conversations on our way back and forth from school.

The woman had her hair plaited all the way down her back and it swung from side to side as she walked. She looked fed up. She had had quite enough. It had been a long way to come and she was having none of this elevated school philosophy. She had not come all this way to listen to such nonsense.

'What does Krishnamurti mean by freedom from thought? The man must be crazy. What freedom is that? Anyway, it is all very well for him to say such things. He has the world at his feet and he can say what he likes. He does not have to go out of his way to earn a living like ordinary people. It is all very well for him.'

Her husband shrugged and made a gesture of despair as he followed behind her, disconsolate.

'Satish has to live in the real world. He cannot always depend on you or your wonderful philosophy. Also, what will happen when he returns home? How is he going to make sense of the world and cope with the pressures of everyday life?' she emphasised again.

They passed out of my hearing, and my sister and I ran off home. I could hear the flip-flops of their footwear amid the receding rumble of the monologue, and then there was silence. The water pump was humming steadily from the large well near the bullock yard. An uneasy feeling came over me as I walked uphill towards home. I felt suddenly estranged from my familiar environment.

The world was a very large place. I was always being reminded by the guests that we were only a small part of it – just a curiosity, as a matter of fact. It was easy to become complacent here, they implied. Many people came and went from different parts of the world, and they often marvelled at the tranquillity of the place. We in return treated them as a curiosity, as we were intrigued by their sense of fashion and their eccentric views on religion, politics, science, psychology – even their approach to the East/West dichotomy which translated into the way they spoke, the manners they assumed and their airs of refinement.

However, it was a little unusual to hear anyone being so outspokenly dismissive of Krishnaji. However, they were not completely unfamiliar sentiments. I had grown up hearing numerous reservations implied by half-finished sentences and shrugs of resignation when staff and relatives came together for social occasions or encountered each other in the grounds. No one really believed that education could bring about a transformation of consciousness. It was generally believed that transformation was a gift from heaven, the domain of an exclusive, deserving few. It was naive to believe otherwise, everyone agreed, but they also thought that the school was certainly a wonderful place in which to live and work.

Freedom from thought, I pondered. What exactly did Krishnaji mean by that? He was fond of saying that thought is limited, yet I was not too sure about that. He said knowledge is limited, and I realised that was true. There was clearly little I knew about the world yet that did not pose a special problem for me except when it came to sitting exams. But thought was not limited, I was sure, since I had examined that for myself. As far as I could see, I could think on and on. I could think and think and think, wracking my brains as I went along.

But there was really no point in thinking like that since it had no relevance to where I was or what I was doing in the moment, whether talking with people, walking, sitting or even climbing trees. This endless inner chatter went on. These questions on the nature of thought itself were a huge distraction, and I kept head-butting the same old thoughts and inflaming my brain. I can see now that it really was a tedious pastime, and what a very unwholesome way to live.

As far as I could determine, thinking fruitlessly in this manner was a waste of time, but I could not seem to stop it. I used to think that if I could win a record for thinking endlessly, I could see some point in it. It was cold comfort, I decided, that after all the fine effort I had put into observing thought, I had come out with nothing. Why should anyone want to think infinitely, and further, what was the point of being free from the clutches of thought?

I envied the woman her determination, her certainty and the power of her convictions. I wished I could walk away in a huff with the same haughty self-assurance and leave all the heavy philosophy behind. It was hard enough just to keep my cool cramming for my Year 10 exams at the end of term.

The motor in the well hummed on, soothing me as I watched the bullocks lying under large tamarind trees, peacefully chewing their cud. Their ears flapped languidly back and forth to discourage flies from settling in their dreamy eyes. I envied their serenity and the nonchalant absence of strife in their lives.

One part of my education required me to observe thought; another part demanded that I use it cleverly to prove how good I was at remembering 'right' information. Observing thought helped to put my limited knowledge in perspective. Yet pursuing correct answers, or finding knowledge, filled my mind with uncertainty and the desire to know even more. It turned my mind into an echo chamber, burgeoning with a longing for peace. The search for knowledge was an insatiable desire, I realised – part of the fabric of thought that swathed my mind with reams of information year after year. Goodness knew what for. I had to take the elders' word for it and trust that all the information would come in good some day. It was a deplorable situation but there was no way out, and unlike the woman in the silk sari, who seemed well-established in life and was making choices for her grandchildren, I had nowhere else to go.

I wondered where I could go after my Year 10 exams. What would I do with my life – and whether I would ever have the freedom of thought beyond the accumulation of knowledge that Krishnaji talked so much about.

Perhaps this freedom might come from the direct perception of life. I could only hope.

Fledgling Love

I had reserved a book in the school library called The Awakening of Intelligence by Jiddu Krishnamurti. It was the biggest book of his that I had seen on the shelves and I was intrigued. As I walked up the tarred road to pick it up, I found myself behind a couple who were heading towards the school's dining hall.

'Life is impossible,' the woman declared. She had big round eyes and wore thick black eyeliner. Her face was heavily made up but she did not have a bottu on her forehead.

'He always had low self-esteem. I built him up so he could stand on his own no matter where he went – and he falls in love with this girl whose gums pop out every time she smiles. At first I thought it was a passing affair, but then it went on for one year, two years and now I can't see an end to it. What if they want to get married? What kind of grandchildren will we have? With his square jawline and her bulging gums, the grandkids will be done for.'

Her husband cleared his throat and suggested that perhaps it was just fledgling love and maybe she was working herself into a state over something that would never eventuate.

'That is all very well for you to say.' The woman's words erupted as she hastened her pace to get away from him.

As I was walking along with them, I couldn't help but overhear their conversation, and I was impressed that the husband had the temerity to speak up against her assertions. Krishnamurti had been speaking that morning about putting order into our lives. I had to admit that the world was a mess when it came to politics, the economy, poverty and the individual lives of people I knew in my own life, and there didn't seem any sign of things changing in a hurry. So the conversation was a welcome break from my bleak thoughts.

Since I was a complete stranger to the middle-aged couple, they did not take any notice of me. They had encountered a pressing problem and were not particularly worried about being overheard. I had no idea who they were talking about and I could not recall anyone in the school whose gums popped out when they smiled. I ran my tongue over my gums and wondered what it might feel like to have such a smile. It was an unpleasant thought and I crinkled my nose in discomfort.

'What I can't understand is, where is his aesthetic sense? All this talk about beauty, natural order, the immeasurable ... and doesn't this school teach them to appreciate beauty? When you hear about communing with nature and wholesomeness, you would expect some of this talk would rub off on the kids. But he goes and falls in love with a girl like that!'

The husband looked at his wife sideways and hesitated before stating the obvious.

'He isn't exactly eye-catching, you know. Neither was I at his age.'

His wife looked back at him with scant respect, as if she was thoroughly perplexed by his lack of sensitivity. She walked on a pace or two, making a dismissive gesture with her manicured fingers as she adjusted the folds of her silk sari over her shoulder and walked on assertively. I watched, fascinated, as her red nail polish glistened. She was wearing a green sari with a red border, and the red of her nail polish matched the border exactly. Unlike the village folk working in the estates, she wore plenty of gold jewellery round her neck and wrists. She did not behave like a regular housewife but seemed to be a woman of independent means. From their language, it was clear that they were both obviously well-educated. She appeared astute and confident, and spoke her mind without mincing her words. I was impressed by her show of determination, and wondered if she was involved in politics like Mrs Indira Gandhi. Then I winced at the thought because the political scene was not too bright, with emergency rule and threats of religious rivalry commanding the daily newspaper headlines.

'The fact is that in matters of the heart, we have little say. I wish you'd realise that so you won't stir up a storm and then simply go away. He has his Year 10 exams to deal with at the end of the year. It won't do to destabilise him right now.

'They are just young adolescents. What do you expect?' her husband continued to caution as he hurried after her, making emphatic but beseeching gestures with his hands in the hope that she would glance back at him. His wife looked away pointedly, casting a disdainful look at the laundry yard where rows of colourful clothes from the girls' hostels were drying in the sun.

I watched the garments flutter in the breeze blowing through the valley. It rarely rained in our part of the world, so although large cumulonimbus clouds were sailing overhead, there was little cause for worry as far as the laundry folk were concerned. They lived in a row of tiny houses at the end of the yard behind some tall shrubs which screened their homes from the road. As the school grew from a few dozen children to many hundreds, more family members were recruited from the village to help with the growing workload. The couple walking ahead of me did not notice the people working on the washing stones at the end of the yard because they were still so immersed in their own conversation.

'I think that after Year 10, we should take him back to Bangalore with us,' the woman continued. 'He can do his Plus 2 in the local college and get used to the ways of the world, instead of muddling around with all this fine philosophy.'

The husband shrugged as if he was familiar with her line of thinking. He glanced up at the clouds, which were heading for the horizon where the blue hills met the wide open sky. His wife was an elegant woman, fair-skinned and fine-featured, with long black hair tied neatly in a bun at the nape of her neck. He was stocky and dark with an unmistakable air of self-assurance about him. I looked at them carefully to see if I could figure out from their appearance if they were related to one of my classmates. I was in Year 10 too and I could not imagine whom they were related to. The valley was full of visitors at this time of year because Krishnamurti was staying with us on his annual trip around India to visit the schools he had established in order to set the scene for a radical revolution in education. I watched the couple as they turned the corner, and wondered if their marriage had been arranged by their family. Perhaps the lady was just projecting her fears, imagining things and worrying extensively about them. Unlike her husband, she was looking straight down, fully engrossed in her thoughts, as she walked ahead of him. Occasionally she looked his way to make sure that he was listening to her. I listened to her leather slippers flapping emphatically against the soles of her feet as she disappeared into the distance.

It was always the same, I thought. It always puzzled me how people came and saw what they wanted to see. From time to time, I had been surprised by the different reactions people had to the valley. On some days, walking past the old and new guest houses, I would hear the guests say radically different things about the set-up. Most of them thought the school was too idyllic, and by being educated here, we students would all flounder once we came into contact with reality. The reality check that I was told I would encounter in the big wide world bothered me. I wondered what I would do with my life once I left Rishi

Valley. Deep in my heart I wanted to be a vaidya, like my grandfather. But I could not bring myself to admit it openly because it seemed such an old-fashioned thing to head for in this modern age, especially after learning to speak English so well. I would have to learn Malayalam all over again and go to a medical college in Thiruvananthapuram, the capital city of Kerala. I did not know if my parents would be able to afford to send me to college to study ayurveda and I did not wish to put them under pressure by mentioning it now.

As I walked up the steep incline past the post office, I recalled the numerous times I had walked along that dust-covered road. I had encountered so many issues that concerned people and mulled over so many problems while walking on this path. These days most of my thoughts were on the subjects I was studying, as I had to do a fair bit of cramming to get past the exams. I could feel my mind bucking like a mule at the tedium of it all. It was extraordinary how many concerns over the various topics crowded my mind as I sought listlessly for some respite from the monotony of remembering facts. The contradictions between a holistic approach to education and the conventional approach rankled in my mind. Yet, I knew that unless I did well in my exams, my future would be limited, so getting things off by heart was the way to go. Increasingly, Krishnamurti's caution to observe was falling on deaf ears, I realised. We had all begun to knuckle down to the serious business of improving our grades.

Once the exams were over, I would be heading back to Kerala, which was a wealthy state compared to the rest of India. I vaguely knew the whereabouts of the college I would join later in the year. A dog barked from the boys' hostels to my right. Life seemed increasingly meaningless if after all these years of studying, I was going to enrol in a new course and study some more. It was as if I had spent my whole life heading for something whereas Krishnamurti was always arresting our attention to the here and now. That was essentially the difference between his view of education and the way the world viewed it. For

Krishnamurti, the whole of life was in the instant, in the present and eminently observable. I felt I was always learning from the fountainhead of creation, and when we spent time with him there was no doubting the fact that life existed in the fullness of the moment. Somehow, in his presence, it was hard to ignore this fact. For years I had kept that in view and yet increasingly, as the pressure of exams weighed on my mind, I could feel his assurance dwindling into a distant dream.

When I left this place all the emphasis on holistic intelligence would change – or would it? For years I had watched him holding the inevitable at bay, urging us on to explore the implications of living according to prescribed ways laid down by society, and religious and political institutions. He had often warned us about blindly following what was said. Institutions were all too contradictory and fragmented to look after our welfare. He had asked us to learn by watching how our minds chose to harbour certain thoughts and feelings and became increasingly entangled in self-centred activity. He had insisted that we observe our own habitual patterns of thought to discover the limitations of thinking. Yet I had to admit that when it came to the rest of my life, I was at the mercy of the larger world. Here was I with my head full of useless information, soon to be at the mercy of some faceless examiner who would put me in a box to be judged as fitting for a particular course. It was an unsavoury thought, and no matter how hard I tried, nothing I could call to mind made any sense anymore. My head was simply teeming with ideas, and the pressure building within was immense.

'Where is the wisdom in relying on the limited to explain the limitless?' I asked myself, understanding for the first time what Krishnamurti had suggested over and over again, seeing how my thoughts were hell-bent on interpreting life within the confines of what I already knew. I was forever struggling and striving to make a coherent whole from the fragments of information I had gathered over the years. That had become the usual pattern, the course my thoughts usually took these days.

Suddenly there was a pause in my thinking and I stood rooted to the spot as I realised that yet again I had come full circle. Perhaps there is simply no way out. Subjecting life to thought always committed the mind to race round the closed circuits of foregone conclusions. Perhaps that is why Krishnamurti never missed a chance to point to the limitations of thought.

And yet that was simply not good enough for me. I always wanted to stretch my imagination further, to come up with some plausible answer to the really big questions that filled my mind. I simply did not wish to stop thinking. I could not stop, I told myself, bridling with righteous indignation. What if the answer was lurking just around the corner, or could that merely be more wishful thinking?

Feeling rather envious, I remembered the woman's assertive stride as she headed towards her midday meal. I could feel my own feet dragging as I walked along the dusty road. Could I really muster enough courage to face the unknowns looming in my not-too-distant future with the same assurance she displayed? I had to admit that, with the way the world was – with its petty politics, wars and depressing lack of equality between people everywhere – there was little I could really look forward to on leaving the valley for good. I was determined to read the new Krishnamurti book in the library before I left the school, in the hope that it would settle my emerging disquiet and help me make sense of the world.

I never did find the girl with the protruding gums, nor the boy who was in love with her. But I wished them luck from time to time.

And then there was Christopher

On my way back from class at Rishi Valley School, heading for lunch, I found myself walking beside a young Australian in his late twenties. He was dressed in blue jeans and a pale blue checked shirt. We were walking past the post office towards my home alongside a mango grove. He had a bounce in his step and was clearly enthralled by the place, whereas I had spent most of the day in the library studying for my Year 12 exams which were due a few months after my eighteenth birthday. My head was aching, dense with economics, commerce and national 'five year plans', with their goals, achievements and success ratios. I had no space left in my head to admire anything. But we were heading in the same direction, so we fell into step along the road to Rishi Konda.

'G'day,' he said. 'What a great place to work. Have you been here for long?'

I was taken aback because I had no idea how he knew my nickname. Only my friends called me 'Geeday' and I had never met him before. I was wearing a sari unlike the other senior students and I realised that he thought I was a member of staff. I wondered if I should set him right or simply smile and let things pass.

Casting about for something else to say, I wished my head would clear so I could engage in a witty conversation instead of churning over Mrs Gandhi's incomprehensible five year plans. He seemed rather nonplussed by my lack of response, and I decided to throw caution to the winds and have a little fun. He had been genuine in his introduction and was probably wondering why I hadn't taken him seriously. I wondered if I had been too off-hand. Not wishing to hurt his feelings, I smiled in apology and fell into step beside him. He was in an expansive mood and eager to learn all about the place.

'I come from Sydney, Australia,' he persevered.

I said that was an interesting name because in my language 'sydh-iney' could be loosely translated to mean 'the essence is now'. Then I regretted I had mentioned the 'now' for fear he would launch into a philosophical inquiry, as I was simply not up to a serious conversation. Trying to avert the inevitable, I explained that my home town was called Mayyanad, and I wasn't working at the school as he had first assumed but I would be completing my studies in a few months.

'Mayya!' he exclaimed. I wonder why people are always talking about 'illusion' in India. This is all so real to me.' He swung around on his heel, throwing open his arms and moving in a complete circle to indicate the environment around him.

We had been walking down a slope towards the gully which curved past the old guesthouse where Krishnamurti would stay when he visited our school. I slowed down, concerned that this young man would slip on the slope as he strode along with a bounce in his step. I had skidded on that particular incline many times as I was growing up.

I was really hungry and dreaded having to talk about enlightenment or being in the now, so I was wishing he would bounce off on his way towards the dining hall or wherever he was going. But he continued to keep pace with me while talking about his impressions of the Deccan Plateau. He told me his name was Christopher.

'The rocks!' he said, 'The shapes of the large granite boulders strewn on the slopes of the surrounding hills ... it's unbelievable. What an ancient magical place.'

Indicating toward the old guesthouse, Christopher told me how he had first come across Krishnamurti's 'teachings'. He'd been walking past the reception desk in a youth hostel in Athens when he heard two travellers talking about Krishnamurti. He had questioned them and they had given him a brochure advertising some upcoming public talks in Brockwood Park, a Krishnamurti centre in Hampshire, England, due to commence two days later.

'Now that was a sign,' he said fervently, his blue eyes sliding back into nostalgia. After reading the brochure, he'd immediately gathered his things, checked out of the hostel and taken a series of buses from Athens to England. The first time he'd heard Krishnamurti speak in Brockwood Park had changed his life, he said. It was as if Krishnamurti was examining and speaking about his own mind; as if his mind had opened and every word seemed to be spoken directly to him. It had been a wonderful coincidence. After that he had travelled overland to India to see how Krishnamurti related with the children at his schools. He had been so impressed. How fortunate I was to have such a teacher, he enthused. I did not share his enthusiasm because my final exams loomed large in my head, but I mustered a polite smile just to keep the conversation going.

I was a little concerned for him as I could see that his imagination was soaring. Thinking he might be overcome by his passion, I tried to bring him down to earth. He was several years older, but unlike me, he was full of life.

'I don't know about that,' I said, trying to sound level-headed. 'I've been listening to Krishnaji for years but he only stays here for a few weeks each year and after that the school goes back to normal.'

But there was no kerbing his excitement. It was evident that he was on a roll and he wasn't quite finished.

'But even to hear him once in a lifetime is so special. If I had not come across his writings, I would never have made sense of my life.'

I looked at him intently, a little taken aback by his honesty. It seemed such a dramatic thing to say to someone on a first encounter.

Christopher's father had died of a heart attack when he was fourteen, he told me. So he'd joined the army straight after he'd finished school. He couldn't think of anything else to do, he said, and besides his dad had been a war veteran, so it seemed like the right thing to do.

I couldn't find it in my heart to stem the tide of words any further as I could hear the sincerity in his voice. I could see that Krishnamurti had turned Christopher's life around, just as it had for many others I had listened to on that road to Rishi Konda. I could sense that I was not taking part in a polite conversation any more. So I listened, feeling rather naive and immature. I had no idea why people became so intense about Krishnamurti's teachings. So often I could not match their intensity. I would watch as their eyes misted over and they stumbled over words, trying to express how much it had meant to them to be able to meet Krishnamurti in person.

Krishnamurti, on the other hand, had implied that we need not read all his books. He had often assured us that it was enough just to pay attention instead. It was sufficient to watch our own thoughts so we would learn about ourselves. I hesitated before mentioning this to Christopher. He waved it aside and continued with his story.

He had gone to Scots College, which was one of the best private schools in Sydney. After school, he had completed a degree at the Royal Military College in Canberra. But he'd resigned after reading a book by Krishnamurti, he said, because his thinking suddenly changed. It hadn't been an easy transition, he confided, but at last here he was.

Christopher was obviously entranced by the place, and commented on the care that had gone into planning what he called 'an enchanting environment for children'. It was as if time had stood still in the valley while, elsewhere, the human race was engaged in a modern rat race. Everything here was so quiet, so tranquil, that he couldn't believe it, he told me. The Deccan Plateau was nothing like anything he had seen in Australia, and the people could have stepped straight out of ancient times.

He spoke with admiration about the landscape being timeless, but I was not sure it was a compliment. I rather enjoyed the feeling of being part of the twentieth century, but I sensed he was talking about the damage the hectic pace of life had on people in the big cities. In movies and documentaries, life looked rosy in the West. But from speaking to foreigners, I picked up the feeling that they bore an enormous weight of suffering. Many of their lives had been touched by the scars of wars and political and economic unrest that they'd lived through. I told him about an Englishman, Mr Moorhead, who had been my neighbour here in India when I was younger, and he too had been a war veteran. Mr and Mrs Moorhead had now returned to England and they had offered me a scholarship to Brockwood, our sister school in Hampshire, I informed him. After the exams I was taking a gap year to study there.

Christopher had loved Brockwood, he told me enthusiastically. He was sure I would have a great time there. After hearing Krishnamurti speak at Brockwood, he had followed him through Europe all the way to India, even driving a huge truck through Afghanistan. It was an extraordinary journey. He described the people as elegant and the landscape spectacular. Now he had some big decisions to make, he said, and he would travel through India for a year or more to visit the many interesting places he had read about recently.

We parted company, going our separate ways. He was lucky he could take time off to travel, I thought, a little enviously. His gratitude to Krishnamurti and high esteem for all that he'd achieved made me feel somewhat daunted by what lay ahead in my life.

Ever since my Year 10 exams and now with Year 12 coming up, the last two years had taken the wind out of my sails, so that I had no inclination to enthuse about anything. The tension at the nape of my neck was unbearable and, sadly, only too familiar. I had lost all sense of composure as I found myself facing an uncompromising world, so that I anticipated a life full of middling compromises if I had to proceed on a course set up by society's norms.

If this is what it takes to live, I thought bleakly, it isn't going to be much of a life. Sad it had all come to this, I thought, as I shifted my armload of books to relieve my aching shoulders. I had grown accustomed to a frightful din in my brain and could only hope that things might settle down after the exams. I longed for some reassurance. Feeling rather humbled by the circumstances of Christopher's life, I began to appreciate how protected we had been as students at the Krishnamurti school. And I could understand a little better why Krishnamurti meant so much to people visiting from overseas.

As I bade Christopher farewell, I wondered whether all the philosophical enquiries I had engaged in would help me face the challenges of the future. What on earth did Krishnamurti really mean by the words 'the future is now'? After all, the future was no trivial matter. I'd felt impelled to ask myself that question many times before.

The very first time I had heard Krishnamurti say those words I had been aged seven, and I had simply tensed and held my breath to observe the next moment emerging as 'the future'. As each moment dawned, I had observed it with exquisite attention. But since then the landscape had changed immensely inside my mind, so that now time stretched far into the distance.

After all this endless study and no matter how many facts I could recall, I realised that my future was still cloaked in mystery. Thinking back to the sense of wonder that had filled my sight every time I walked the road as a child, I looked about me again now. I couldn't see much because my head felt so dense with information. My body was tense with a desire to be right at all times, and facts and figures sprang to mind with incredible alacrity.

My thoughts were no longer attuned to the flow of information through my senses. As I looked inward, I saw that, instead, my mind resembled an arena where a merciless matador flagged his red cape and I charged at it like a blinded bull.

Christmas Day 1980

My mother and I were standing by the well as she looked me over in dismay. I was transgressing all the conventions that she had upheld throughout her life, yet I had the courage to be still standing there. A strange mixture of outrage and then dawning respect arose in her gaze, which surprised me.

My heart was breaking for her as I did not enjoy turning into her worst nightmare. I had not set out to challenge all the notions she had upheld during her life. We were facing each other by the well. Her curly hair was knotted at the nape of her neck. She had been cooking in the kitchen and had stepped out to bathe before heading off for work. I watched the angle of her neck as she looked down at the blue sky reflected in the pool of water at the bottom. We peered at our reflections and remained speechless, thinking of the many times we had done this together over my lifetime. I glanced sideways at the sweet contours of her ear, the soft curve of her cheek and her broad dark forehead in profile. I regretted that she was so stricken. I had never seen her lose her poise like this before.

She had done nothing to deserve the pain and uncertainty that I was inflicting on her, and I knew that she would have to endure years of humiliation and become the laughing stock of her community. People would probably ostracise her and not invite her to weddings and functions for years.

She had worked and supported her maternal family since she was sixteen. She had helped educate her younger siblings. She had done all that was required of her to win the respect and regard of her peers, and here was I casting a shadow on her life. She was clearly taken aback at my resolve – but I had to remain resolute.

'We've invested so much in your education ... for this?' she asked at last, her voice strangled in disbelief.

I let the words come, hoping to defray the tension. Anything to ease her pain. In my stomach was a tight knot of anguish as I swallowed hard and held my peace. Uncertainty, I thought, so much uncertainty ... and yet in the throes of all this there was a ruthless determination on my part, knowing that I could not, would not, subject myself to the constraints that had governed her life. Nothing seemed to exist for her besides what people would say and think.

Having watched my thoughts for years, I wondered why that should matter so much to her. Why did she hold others' views in such high regard? What was the big deal? I could think all kinds of things about people. It often had no bearing on truth, but I still enjoyed thinking those thoughts anyway. I had been doing this all my life and I could see how fallible my constructs were. Sometimes I had surprised myself at the adroit manoeuvres of my own imagination. I was capable of convincing myself of anything to uphold a particular point of view. During the dialogues we had once a week in class, I had watched many of my friends do the same. So why was she so concerned about what other people thought of her?

Perhaps she hadn't looked at it that way. She had led a conventional life, governed by the codes and ethics of her time, whereas I wished to marry outside my caste, my community and my country.

I would be embracing customs and values that were incomprehensible to civilised society, she said.

She couldn't even conceive of such a life. Why was I running after it? What did I think I was doing?

'What of the divorce rate in the West? I hear that no one stays married there for very long,' she warned, hoping to dissuade me.

They are very real facts – statistics that were carefully put together by educated people. They can't lie, she said. Indulgence and promiscuity were the hard facts of life in the West. Did I really wish to take on such a challenge?

I looked away quickly, feeling perturbed. Then she tried another tack. We are all influenced by our cultures. What made me think I could pull it off on my own? The two of us would have nothing in common. Arranged marriages worked, she insisted, because we all had a shared culture, shared values and codes of behaviour to rely on during times of stress and upheaval. Such times come in everyone's life, she added, looking at me anxiously. No one is spared challenges in life. Only a reliable community with sound values could ensure a stable lifestyle.

And what made me think that God would smile on a match of my own choice? She wouldn't be around to guide me or help me during difficult times. No one would lift a finger to help if something went wrong, considering I had scorned all the customs sanctioned by our community. Why should they bother? I would be out there on my own fending off the pressures of a promiscuous, arrogant society.

My heart was pounding in my chest. I wished she would just leave me alone for a while. Besides, everything she claimed added to the reasons why I could never marry into her community. Their level of apprehension and dire predictions with regard to life made me nervous, and most of the time I felt stifled, constrained by their projection of the norm, their circumspect behaviour, their conventions and adulations. I didn't care if things didn't work out in the end. At least I would have had a say in my own life. Anything would be better than marrying traditionally to keep everyone else happy. I did not wish to win respect that way. I found it an appalling prospect.

Looking at the anxiety in her eyes, I realised how very real her fears for me were. Clutching my hands, I looked around at the yard to see where I could go and then I began to cry. Feeling the tears rolling down my cheeks, I ran past her to our room, and she hastily stepped aside. I collapsed into a corner of the room, squashing myself against the wall beside my bed, and straining my back and shoulders for some support. It was comforting to feel the cool concrete floor I was sitting on. My head felt hard and hot as I clutched it with both hands, trying to suppress the chaos erupting within.

I was not at all afraid for myself but I felt a deep anguish for the pain and humiliation she would have to face. Squirming in the corner, I was glad for the seclusion and darkness of my room. Nothing had prepared me for the dread I had seen in her face. She had no control – that was part of it. What could be so frightening to warrant such a reaction? I hadn't set out deliberately to hurt her. Things had just worked out that way.

'Twenty years I have worked for these kids,' I heard her confiding to her older sister. 'He comes dancing into my life all the way from Australia and sweeps my child from my arms.'

'Careful what you say to her,' her sister cautioned. Her own daughter had committed suicide at fifteen after enduring months of malicious rumours about her good character. She had been a beautiful girl and many young men in the neighbourhood had admired her.

'Besides, she is not a child anymore. It is her life. At least she is alive and healthy, and they are following the proper channels of betrothal. Be grateful for that. Let her be. She might grow out of it, you never know. Besides, it is probably best she marries him now, since the news has spread like wildfire all over the countryside. I told you not to give the girls too much freedom, but you have always been headstrong. At least be thankful she is not pregnant. He may be from Australia, but he is a healthy young man and many would consider him a great catch.'

There was a long pause as they carried on a muted conversation. I sat tense against the corner, feeling the pain in my chest and an erratic pulse all the way to the top of my head. My aunt had never been a favourite of mine, but I realised that her concern for my mother was genuine. For the first time in my life I was grateful to her. Wiping my eyes on a white cotton cloth, I listened to their low voices as they walked away from the well towards the front yard.

I could hear the brooding chicken clucking in the yard. There was a cuckoo calling from the mango tree and then there was silence. Through the window I watched a copper-tone bird balance itself upside down on a palm frond as it pecked at the leaves. It was a fine balancing act. The long black tail feathers, lined with streaks of white, splayed out to hold the bird's rust-coloured body in place while it fed on insects that I could not see, hidden under the palm leaves. Sunlight glanced across the palm fronds, glistening with the bird's every move. There was so much going on in life at any given moment since the whole of life was condensed into an instant. It was really remarkable, if one cared to consider such things. It was well worth marvelling at, I thought, except for the pressing circumstances I found myself in. No matter how hard I tried to look at these impressions, my thinking stopped short at the same spot, unable to go any further than realising the fact that thought takes time whereas life is immeasurable.

I was glad that I had made a decision that was going to change my life forever. It had taken a great deal of soul-searching on my part. Now thanks to my older cousin who had rashly taken her own life over similar circumstances, it seemed my extended family was not going to stand in my way. That made things a lot easier. As I wondered if I was doing the right thing, I realised that I could be sure only after the event. I thanked my cousin in my heart, where she still lived amid the memories of our childhood spent running together around the yards chasing after the chickens, a cat and stray dogs from our special places, 'pineapple springs' all the way to 'the black hole'. I remembered with some nostalgia the wonderful stories she had told us of gods and demons and celestial beings, just as she had taught us to do cartwheels and somersaults along the sandy road to the paddy fields. She would have been present at my wedding if it hadn't been for the malicious gossip that had incited her to take her own life.

The enormity of her action had not really sunk in at the time since I had been eight when she took her life. Now, twelve years later, looking at my own life stretching way ahead of me, I fully understood what a shock it had been for her family.

We had all lost out on that day. My aunt had never been the same after her daughter's suicide, and now that I came to think of it, neither had my mother. It was something that none of us spoke about; a sorrow that was too painful for us to own, let alone explore with the open-hearted honesty that Krishnamurti brought to any topic, however pressing.

If my marriage went ahead as I'd planned, it would break down conventions and, in a small community like ours, would create new boundaries. Tongues would wag yet again but as I listened in surprise to the two sisters, I realised that they were not going to let anyone destroy their children this time. They were going to support me and stand by me, giving me their tacit consent. That was all I needed.

Rather than hold the wedding in my home town, Mayyanad, as tradition might have dictated, my parents decided we would be married near Rishi Konda in Andhra Pradesh, where Christopher and I had met.

We married two months later on Christmas Day, 1980. Our wedding ceremony was performed in an ancient temple in Thettu, a village at the base of Rishi Konda, to the west of Rishi Valley. It was an auspicious day, the priest said, for the East and West to come together in marriage. Looking at our birth charts, he proclaimed that we had nine matches out of ten for a successful partnership. The news was received with gratitude by my parents.

'After all, going so far away to fend for herself, she will need all the help she can muster,' they muttered to each other with wry humour.

I could tell they were relieved. Consenting to that particular date, and the Christmas spirit that went with it, was their parting gift for my seemingly foolhardy but surprisingly successful life venture. At the end of the ceremony we all walked in a circle around the temple carved out of granite boulders from Rishi Konda. The villagers gathered around to give us their blessings.

Notes

Edava

The mind is highly sensitive to the flow of information through the senses, and there is a smooth transference of wisdom from one generation to the next.

The Consulting Rooms

Education comes in many forms in daily life. This story is about the curiosity of children and their observation of others in learning about the world. Early on, one child learns about disease, bad habits in life and the pragmatics of interfamilial links.

Land of Illusion

A child may not understand why her memory is at odds with what she sees in a 'reality check'. The idea that words can alone uphold truth is clearly undermined by one girl's clear observation of her surroundings.

Learning From the Ground Up

Learning things off by heart is a memorable occasion when a child is trained to take pride in recalling information.

A Rose by any other Name

School is a reflection of the rest of the world, so how one engages at school has profound implications for the rest of one's life. Observing superficially cannot reveal the depth of learning that is possible. A rose from afar is just a splash of colour but on closer examination it gives generously of its perfume.

Beloved of the Gods

Krishnamurti established Rishi Valley School as a caring community to celebrate nature and beauty, enabling children to realise that intelligence is sensitive to verbal and non-verbal cues from a vital and ever-changing environment.

The Sandalwood Tree

What makes a good life? Waking fresh to the world of nature each day or studying for a formal education? Are there benefits in both ways of living? What opportunities lie ahead and how many people are content to live in the moment?

A Common Well
The spontaneous movement of life is broken up in the retelling of it. Observing the difference between a narrative and actuality gives one a deeper understanding of life and the nature of thought.

Salute
Questioning assumptions empowers one to relinquish traditional ways of life, giving rise to a need for vigilance in blindly following conventions, as well as the emergence of a critical awareness of the standards we live by.

Dancing Sticks
Ideas of ambition, fickleness and the value of being pragmatic are tackled in this story. It's important to realise how great the possibilities of life are without overlooking the opportunities for learning intrinsic to every moment.

Who is this I?
A pragmatic resolution of inner conflict occurs in this story. The realisation of 'I' comes as a particular act of recall, so the self is then seen as a mechanical and universal phenomenon.

Freedom in the Hills
A story about awareness of how as children we gradually succumb to pressures of how to be and to present our bodies to the world, causing physical and psychological inhibitions.

The Banyan Tree
The 'tree of knowledge' is the centrepiece of education. In holistic education, scaffolds are in place to nurture the observer in order to shift the emphasis from 'knowing' to learning.

Free Rangers
Freedom sounds great, but the responsibility of doing as one likes comes at a cost. How can words be so misleading?

Role Play
Improvising by using a basket filled with notes of random rules and regulations leaves a marked impression on the mind about the arbitrary role of authority in one's life.

Eavesdrop and Hoodwink

A jaunt into the realms of fantasy yields a lifelong insight into the nature of thought. A child learns about both the world of imagination and the hazards of overlooking the enduring facts of life.

A Suitable School

Education as a subject of study is always in the students' minds at a Krishnamurti school. What is education, transformation, philosophy and freedom of thought? One child recognises that what is normal for her at school is considered radical by many respectable people from outside her known world.

Fledgling Love

Our preoccupations have a strong impact on our outlooks on life. It is amazing to see how two people living together can differ greatly on the same topic. What has this to do with attachment and how does this impact our lives?

And Then There was Christopher

At the very point when life is arduous and confusing, two people with different mindsets might come together to influence each other and gain a unified appreciation of the world.

Christmas Day 1980

How important is it to act with clarity of vision during the course of one's life? Obstacles that might seem insuperable may be easily overcome when people decide to work together in the best interests of all involved.

From the same publisher

ANGELA'S ANOREXIA
The story of my mother

A son's story of the debilitating illness, anorexia nervosa, that his single mother suffered from throughout his childhood. The mother and son formed a close bond and the boy's description of their life together is filled with both joy and sadness. A true story showing the boy's experience of growing up fast in Australia and New Zealand, caring for his mother while coming to understand her sickness and his need to develop an independent spirit early on.

Damian Cooper has written a straightforward, honest and loving account of his boyhood, set against a poignant parallel story of his mother's excessive focus on body image, food, diet and exercise.

Category: SELF-HELP/EATING DISORDERS AND BODY IMAGE

ARCO
The legend of the blue vortex

An exciting new story from first-time novelist, Ferdinando Manzo, Arco explores man's battle with the sea in an attempt to seek solace.
The story is set in two different eras: on the high seas among ancient pirates and in contemporary Europe ravaged by war. The legend of the blue vortex – a door into another world – is the central focus of both periods.

An adventure story, it also raises philosophical questions about love and the purpose of life.

Category: FICTION Magical Realism/Romance/Fantasy

BURMA MY MOTHER And Why I Had to Leave

Myanmar's future is informed by its past - and BURMA MY MOTHER tells it like it is.
A valuable story of living through good times and plenty of bad in Burma, now known as Myanmar, before an escape to a new life of freedom.

Author **Sao Khemawadee Mangrai**'s husband, Hom, was imprisoned for 5 years, and his father was shot and killed sitting alongside independence leader, General Aung San, when he was assassinated.

Khemawadee grew up in a Shan state in the north-east of Myanmar, previously known as Burma, and now lives in Sydney. Her sad memories are also infused by the beauty of the country and the grace of Myanmar's Buddhist culture.

Category: MEMOIR

DRENCHED BY THE SUN

The poetry of Syam Sudhakar draws on his cultural roots in Kerala as well as the splendor of its natural habitat. Palms, green paddy fields, mountain country, tropical downpours, the sun, the sea, shooting stars and even an enchantress all make their appearance. Sudhakar is an award-winning poet writing in English and Malayalam with 5 collections to his credit. He is currently based in Kerala, teaching and researching South Indian poetry.

Category: POETRY

The Road to Mandalay Less Travelled

'The Road to Mandalay Less Travelled' by **Ingrid Raj** provides research on a selection of Anglo-Burmese writing published from the period of British rule up in Burma up until 2007. What Raj shares with us in this study is the knowledge she gained about the value of social resistance achieved through writing. Both fiction and non-fiction texts are included in arguing a case that these might be viewed as tools of often ambivalent resistance against oppressive regimes, both local and colonial. Her research deserves a wider readership than was initially provided, and to this aim Sydney School of Arts & Humanities presents the work as its first publication in this new category of Essays & Theses. We hope that specialist researchers as well as members of the general reading public take this opportunity to learn more about the culture of the people of Myanmar through their unique approach to storytelling, based largely on their religious understanding, their rich store of folk legend and their chequered history.

Category: MEMOIR/LITERATURE/BURMA-HISTORY

Jiddu Krishnamurti World Philosopher Revised Edition

The life of the 20th-century philosopher Jiddu Krishnamurti was truly astonishing. As this new updated edition shows, people from all over the world would gather to hear him speak the wisdom of the ages.

Biographer **Christine (CV) Williams** carried out research over a period of four years to write this ebook account of Krishnamurti's life. She studied his major archive of personal correspondence and talks, and interviewed people who knew him intimately.

Krishna was born into poverty in a South Indian village, before being adopted by a wealthy English public figure, Annie Besant. As an adult he settled in California, travelling to India and England every year to give public lectures that inspired spiritual seekers beyond any single religion.

Category: BIOGRAPHY

www.ingramcontent.com/pod-product-compliance
Lightning Source LLC
LaVergne TN
LVHW041629070426
835507LV00008B/522